And May It Be Well With Your Soul

Joan Eytle Kendall

10,000 blessings to you Sally !
For your deep listening, for being
on the other end of the thread
I have been unravelling, and
for being with me at the start of a
new tapestry. ♡ Joan x

Joan Eytle Kendall

ISBN: 978-1546674368

CONTENTS

PREAMBLE

I am not a doctor, I don't have any medical training; but I am grateful that there is a medical profession. I am a great supporter of our own National Health Service here in the UK, and contribute to the funds of organisations researching new drugs and pioneering new treatments.

I know that medical and surgical interventions help save lives and can improve the quality of life for those with a chronic condition or in the final stages of a terminal illness.

I am happy that our NHS recognises the contribution of psychological, emotional and spiritual therapies to health and well-being, and that some hospitals and GP practices offer an integrated approach to healthcare.

I am not a doctor and I don't have any medical training and so I cannot write this tale from a medical perspective, though without the doctors this particular story could not have been told. However, healing and well-being have been at the core of my exploration for decades, in all of the many roles I have experienced:

As a teacher in schools, supporting the development of young minds. As a community worker, working alongside abused women, empowered to change old patterns. As a social worker, seeking to improve the quality of life and well-being of my clients. As a social work lecturer, sharing experience and knowledge with those, like myself, committed to social justice. As a manager of staff and services in the voluntary sector, committed to policies and practices of inclusion. As a mentor, supporting newly appointed managers to understand and undertake their roles effectively. Supporting groups and individuals to find their own voices and places in society, act with confidence in difficult situations, gain new skills and understanding and make their unique contributions to the world.

As a counsellor, helping people to explore their feelings and emotions to improve their experiences and develop self-awareness. As a massage therapist, aromatherapist and therapeutic healer, supporting clients to address and restore balance in their lives at the physical, psychological, emotional and spiritual levels.

As a doula in a birth centre and privately, supporting women emotionally and practically, enabling them to have the most satisfying and empowered experience that they can during pregnancy, birth and their early days as a new mum.

Most recently, as a metaphysical practitioner supporting people to understand themselves as *spiritual beings having a human experience*; to question and change the thoughts and beliefs that stop them living a balanced and healthy life; and to awaken to a deeper appreciation of the working of Universal Energy that surrounds and flows through us all, connecting us to the One Infinite Intelligence.

I am a mother and a weaver and a storyteller. I have my daughter's blessing. I have excellent credentials for telling this story the way I believe it needs to be told…

The loom is warped
The threads are chosen
The weaving begins
The story unfolds…

To all the mothers and daughters of my line, especially Eunice, Gertrude, Doreen, Tunde & Keso, with love

This story starts long before the teller even knew there was a story to be told. That's the way it is with stories. The beginning is often far before the experience...

Karen Wilson, *Science of Mind*, July 2015

PROLOGUE

As the King of Hearts says in *Alice's Adventures in Wonderland*: 'Begin at the beginning, and go on till you come to the end: then stop...' But as Life is eternal and forever expanding there is really no beginning and no end, we just step into and out of our stories at a particular moment in time and space. This is where I choose to step into the story...

Diary entry: January 27th 2015
Walk, weave, write, wait...
Walk, weave, write, wait...
This has been the rhythm of my life for sometime

Walk, weave, write, wait...
Walk, weave, write, wait...
These are the threads with which my loom is dressed

Walk, weave, write, wait...
Walk, weave, write, wait...
And I have been patient letting Life lead me
But I sense that the waiting is over...

There are several diary entries from September 2014 to January 2015 that tell a tale of something about to unfold, something for which I am preparing...

Diary entry: Tuesday November 11th
Like a woman in her final trimester I am preparing... Bin bags and boxes my companions I answer the call to 'make ready'

Heavier than I want to be but full of energy and anticipation I prepare for the new arrival – this gestation period a lifetime's work. Answering the silent call I work – eager for labour to begin. The waiting will soon be over…

Diary entry: Friday December 12th

I do not wish to deck the hall with boughs of holly
Nor do I believe that this is the season to be jolly
I do not desire artificial light and merriment at this time of year
I welcome the silence and the dark
I enjoy watching the colour drain out of the landscape
Leaving us with the subtle muted tones of green and brown

I crave this same process for myself
A fitting end to the cycle of the year
I envy nature her truth I am not afraid of the dark
I do not wish to deny death his moment of glory
Much within me is ready to be committed to the earth
Dust to dust ashes to ashes
Fighting the man-made light for the right to die

Celebration does not always need a fanfare
Let us keep this for the long fecund days to come
Could we not allow ourselves to rest?
To follow nature's example and empty out lie fallow
Breathe gentle like Mother Earth
And wait…

To Carol and Kim, my fellow textile artists in 'Women of the Cloth', I write:

I have come to the conclusion that I need some space and time to just Be. I feel the need to stop doing and to listen to that inner voice that we spend so much time ignoring or stifling…

I am a member of South London Women Artists, and have taken on a role as one of the curators of an exhibition we have called 'Death and Transition', scheduled for April 2015. I write to my fellow organisers:

> It is with some sadness that I write to let you know that I will be withdrawing from curating the exhibition... I really feel the need to spend some time in 'gentle contemplation', in order to get some clarity about my future direction and priorities...

As always I allow the words to flow, confident that when the time is right all will be revealed...

PART I

1 – FOREBODING

And it was then that in the depths of sleep
Someone breathed to me: 'You alone can do it,
Come immediately.'

Jules Supervielle

Diary entry: Saturday January 3rd
Our youngest has flown the nest
Taken herself off to far flung exotic places
My heart both aches and is filled with joy
To see her take flight and soar
And as she climbs her dazzling heights
I am reminded that I do not have to lose sight of her
I too am free to soar
I have my own journeys to make
And my own dreams to fulfil
We each must follow our hearts
As individualisations of the One Spirit…

Keso's leaving has affected me more than I anticipated. I am not a woman given to smothering mothering, feeling deeply the truth in Kahlil Gibran's words:

Your children are not your children.
They are the sons and daughters of Life's longing for
    itself
They come through you but not from you,
And though they are with you yet they belong not to
    you…

I want my children to follow their hearts and dreams and live as fully as they can. So I am surprised to find myself suddenly tearful at the thought of her, avoiding phoning or FaceTiming because I find the long-distance contact so painful.

I feel that our FaceTime calls are spent peering into the screen, scanning each other's faces for the truth of how we are really feeling. I decide to email Keso:

> *My wonderful Keso I just want you to know that I miss you very much. At the same time I am very excited for you and so happy that you are doing what serves you best in life. You have been an inspiration to me to get on and enjoy life and do the things that bring me pleasure. Bless you for being such an amazing daughter.*

I get a swift reply, which confirms my suspicions:

> *Aw mumma what a lovely message to get on a Friday morning! I miss you very much as well, which is why I keep pestering you to come out here for our birthdays in February! I'm glad you're happy for me – so far I'm having an amazing time but hope you are too. It seems like when we speak you're trying not to seem too sad. I hope you're OK and happy and feel loved because you are! Remember I'm just a phone call away if you want to talk or rant or scream. Sending you lots of love hugs and kisses from the other side of the world.*

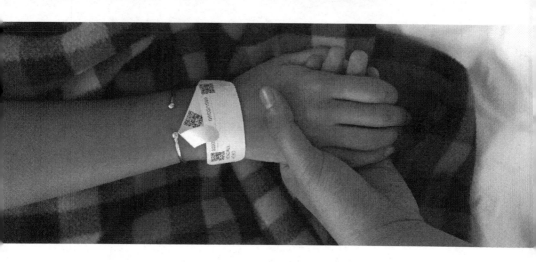

2 – THE DESCENT

*There will come a time when you believe everything
is finished. That will be the beginning...*

Louis L'Amour

I'm afraid that I have not really been following the emails to and fro between father and daughter about her 'cold'. I am aware that the cold has become a sinus infection that is proving difficult to shift, causing her some pain and some time off work. I only begin to engage with it fully when Anthony copies me into an email from her. January 29th:

> *Still very much recovering – the pain got a lot worse over the past couple of days. Went back to the doctor today who thinks it's a bad sinus infection and sent me for some scans. Will get the results tomorrow/Saturday and if so will have to take a course of antibiotics. At least with the scan we'll get to the cause of it. Managed to go to work yesterday and today though not sure how productive I've been! Let's Skype tomorrow/at the weekend...*

Much later Keso describes that time to me:

I've never felt pain like that before and the painkillers which I knew were strong only relieved it for an hour or so, after that I sat counting down the time until I could take the next pill. I wasn't sleeping properly and the fevers were incredible – I'd wake up covered in sweat. By the time I went to see the doctors the pain was terrible but they seemed reluctant to take it more seriously. They both dismissed some of my symptoms – quickly saying that the heat in my head was unrelated and that the sinuses were fine… Maybe if Jay had been around to see the pain I was in and the fevers I was having it would have been different.

Our daughter Keso and her boyfriend Jay have been living together in West London for about six years. They met just before Keso went off on her gap year travels. On her return the relationship became established and we have become very close to the Canlas clan, a warm and welcoming Filipino family. For the past year Keso and Jay have been making plans to move to Hong Kong. A visit the previous Christmas to Jay's sister Jess and brother-in-law Edward, recently moved there for work, had decided them that the time was ripe for adventure. Keso successfully applied for and got the offer of a job with an international PR company with an office in Hong Kong. After two Skype interviews and a visit to their London office it is agreed that she will start work on January 9th.

So it is on a cold Tuesday evening two days before Christmas that Anthony and I take Keso and Jay to Heathrow Airport to catch their Cathay Pacific flight to the Philippines. Possessions have been boxed and shipped; friends and family bid au revoir. Christmas will be celebrated in the Philippines with Jay's parents and family before heading 'home' to Hong Kong and a new life. It is a sad parting although we wish them well and are excited for them.

In the new year Keso and Jay flat hunt in Hong Kong and finally settle on a one-bed newly refurbished apartment on the tenth floor of a block in the lively district of Wan Chai on Hong Kong Island. Jay heads back to the UK for his last weeks at work and to spend time with his parents – who are now losing both children to Hong Kong – with plans to return to Keso in early February. Keso is on her own but happy to have started work, and with furniture ordered from IKEA, she is finding her feet in Hong Kong but eager for Jay to join her.

It is Saturday, cleaning day in our house. The day is bright and cold, I am cleaning the stairs. I am keeping myself busy hoping it will distract me from the pain I am feeling, quite literally, in my heart. What on earth is the matter with me! My eyes are smarting but I am determined not to give in to tears. I am fearful that once I start I will not be able to stop and I can't let others see me crying. So cleaning it is.

Anthony is calling me, he's in the conservatory. Keso is FaceTiming us, he clicks the 'accept' button and a rather grainy Keso fills the screen. We are not prepared for what we see and what we hear. Keso is twenty-five years old, she runs regularly, she does Pilates and yoga, and is a keen tennis player; she eats healthily. Why then is she in tears in a hospital bed telling us that she is in a great deal of pain and paralysed in her left arm and leg? Nothing is making any sense; I see tears, I hear words, but I cannot properly grasp their meaning. Everything around me has disappeared; I am fixated on the grainy image on the screen. Anthony is saying something and between her tears Keso is replying but I can't take it all in. *Lump on my head... left leg gave way in the shower... Jess and Edward to the hospital... CT scan, echo-cardiogram, chest X-ray... can't use my left arm either... acute ward...*

I'm back cleaning the stairs, FaceTime must have ended, where's Anthony? My daughter Tunde is coming downstairs and I sink onto the steps and burst into tears. 'What's up?' she says, studying me. I tell her; she sits down, asks me some sensible questions – she's a midwife – and tells me that Keso is in the right place for us to get some answers, and that I should calm down before I speak to Keso again. I have had my moment of sheer, uncontrollable panic – during the next three months, when things go from bad to unimaginable, it does not return.

Over the course of the afternoon Anthony and I drift together, exchange a few words, make a few observations and continue with our various tasks. We will get Jess's phone number as she is arranging Keso's transfer from Ruttonjee, the public hospital that she was taken to initially, to Hong Kong Adventist, one of the hospitals approved by her work health insurance policy. Has anyone spoken to Jay? Anthony leaves him a message on his mobile. And much later – one of us might need to go. The evening comes and goes each of us deep in our own thoughts. It is safer to say nothing; at times like this it is so easy to imagine the worst, I don't want to give voice to my fears. I conjure up affirmations to replace the unwanted thoughts. I am exhausted from the effort:

All fear and doubt is gone. Love is stronger than any other force in the Universe.

It's gone midnight; Anthony and I are sitting up in bed with the laptop and our passports in front of us. We are checking the availability of flights – just in case. What is the earliest we could be at the airport? 'It's really Sunday morning now' I say, 'it's not realistic to think that we could be at Heathrow before late afternoon.' We find a Cathay Pacific flight that's leaving at 5 pm, getting into Hong Kong around midday on Monday. We have known that with our other commitments only one of us can go, but which one? Anthony holds out the two passports. 'Pick one,' he says. I hesitate, close my eyes and reach for a passport.

I am on my way to Hong Kong.

Stars are the light of lanterns
Held high to guide us through
The deep waters of the soul
If we could see who held them high
We would not fear, we would not feel alone
They form a guard of honour for our journey
'Remember' they whisper 'keep your focus on the Light
As you step into these uncharted seas

And all will be well...'

3 – CHAOS

Here we must deal with awe, fascination, and terror, with
ignorance shot through with the lightning of certainty, and
with feelings of exuberance, love and bliss...
Francis Huxley

Reflections:
I sit in the Silence and imagine that I have been preparing for this moment all of my life. As I reassess my skills, knowledge and experience for the challenges that lie ahead I become more grounded, more certain of the outcome. I know that I am in charge of my thoughts and beliefs, even though I cannot determine the outcome of every circumstance. As the saying goes, 'energy flows where attention goes'. So stop the negative thinking Joan – as soon as I've said it I realise the overwhelming nature of this task. I revise my request. Observe your negative thinking Joan and don't attach to it. Watch it come and go, acknowledge this as a part of the human condition and replace it with more positively productive thoughts. This is harder work than I had ever imagined. It is two years since I completed my training with the Metaphysical Society for the Expansion of Consciousness, but I still feel like a novice with this particular practice. How to avoid consciousness getting caught up in the pain and suffering of what appears to be

unfolding? I breathe into the silence. Snippets of a Mooji satsang come back to me: *don't fall asleep... forces may come to push you off balance, don't give into them, stay in your empty centre... observe the mind but don't go there... stay in the cave of your own heart...*

I am told that the Universe never gives you more than you can handle – and if ever there was a reason to believe this it is here and now. I don't ask the 'why' question; amazingly both Anthony and I have managed to steer clear of it. Intuitively we must know that to go there would be the wrong thing to do. Right now that large metaphysical question that resides in such a small word threatens to overwhelm and immobilise me.

In the Silence it comes to me that there are two ways to take the journey ahead of me. I can think of it as a dark night of the soul, as Thomas Moore calls those moments when we perceive our lives to be falling apart and we are plunged headlong into life's darkest hours. Or I can embrace Rumi's beautiful observation that, 'the wound is the place where the Light enters you'. Adversity, in any of its forms, can bring us to a deeper realisation of ourselves as expressions of the One Universal Power, call it what you will – Source, Presence, Life Force, God, Creative Energy. It is in these times particularly that we are supported to find our power to act.

The Silence is the quiet, empty space within, accessed by paying attention to the breath. Through the breath we remember that there is something greater and more powerful than ourselves that breathes us, over which we have no control. In the Silence we are safe to relinquish ego and open to the unknown.

In his book, *Anam Cara*, John O'Donohue says that poetry is the language of silence, in which you will find cleansing illumination. The poetic style found in places in this book, unattributed, indicates the 'illumination' that came out of my time in the Silence.

In this space of total surrender it is possible to access the indwelling wisdom of Universal Spirit that guides us, and is forever expanding... You can close your eyes and step into the Silence at any time. Become aware of the rhythm of your breathing and the sensations in your body. Allow thoughts to come and go; if you feel in danger of attaching to them return your awareness to the rhythm of your breathing. Trust that here you will find the answers to your questions...

In the Silence it has been decided – ours is a sacred journey. We are headed to the Light...

4 – ARRIVAL

And suddenly you know... its time to start something new and trust the magic of beginnings

Anon

I have arrived in Hong Kong, that vertical city as Jay calls it. It's February 1st 2015, and I've been twelve and a half hours in the air. My mind is a jumble of thoughts that come and go. It's tiring work being consciously observant, and inevitably anxious and fearful thoughts slip in under the wire and exhaust me. My body aches from being so still for so long; when released from the confines of the plane it strides out purposefully more from a desire to be fully operational than from any planned activity. But my spirit is strong; I know what I am here to do, I am eager to see my daughter.

> We are a gift to the world. Spirit saw fit to incarnate Itself as us in form, so it is incumbent upon us to use all of our gifts and talents to live life to the fullest.
>
> Rev. Patti Paris

I feel that this is the way to approach the days ahead. I am here to use my gifts and talents so that Keso has the opportunity to live life to the fullest.

Jess meets me at the airport, we hug and I sense that she is as glad to see me as I am to be here. She hands over my Octopus travel card and we begin the high-speed journey to Hong Kong Island. There is much building work and land reclamation underway. Hong Kong's vertical outline changes almost monthly, but despite the constant and rapid urban development, almost 70 per cent of the total area of Hong Kong is made up of countryside. Forty per cent of the land is classified as 'protected areas', which includes country parks, special sites and conservation areas. I learn this over the course of my three-month stay through reading, talking to those who live here and personal observation. But right this moment none of this is of much interest to me.

Out of the airport express and into a taxi. 'Is it far?' I ask Jess – please don't let it be far! I discover over the next few weeks that nowhere in Hong Kong is far, on foot or otherwise. It is midday, traffic is not as yet heavy, and we make it to the hospital in fifteen minutes. Jess is an easy companion, she talks to me so that there are no awkward silences and I know she is sharing lots of information with me, but I can't take much in, I need to see my daughter.

We take the lift to the third floor and Jess points to a room. I slowly and cautiously push the door open, peeping around it tentatively. 'Hello, my love!' I say softly and tenderly, 'I am so happy to see you!' I wrap her in my arms as best I can, stroke her cheeks, kiss her, search for her hand and kiss that too, realising that it takes quite an effort to raise it to my lips – it is her left hand. She looks pale and weak. 'Oh Mumma, I am so glad you are here, what's happening to me!' 'You're getting plenty lovin' from me,' I say, choosing to ignore the real meaning of her question for now. In truth I don't have the answer for her. She is being sorely tested, that much I know, but this isn't what she needs to hear. I take her in; her plentiful head of hair is in great disarray, spread out in a tangled mass on the pillow. I can't see the lump, but I know it's there. She's very pale-looking, very thin and sad in her hospital pyjamas, and she's just a bit too long for the bed. I remember the texts and FaceTime conversations we have had, Keso urging me to 'come in February, Mumma, we can celebrate our birthdays together!' And my reply 'I'd love to, but what will I do with gran-gran?' Well it seems that Keso has had her way, for here I am!

Gran-gran, as she is known in the family, is my 91-year-old mother. She has a diagnosis of progressive dementia, and she lives with us. Our lives are organised around her growing needs, and it is becoming more and more difficult for Anthony and I to lead the independent and spontaneous lives we once did.

The journey has started, I tell myself. I am reminded of Mooji's words: 'Mind and body have taken the journey but the real home-place is your own heart.' Although Keso and I have not had the 'what's-the-meaning-and-purpose-of-Life' conversation, we've touched upon it at those times when she's felt vulnerable and alone, and she's been a witness to and support through my own dark night of the soul. She knows my life-long commitment to self-knowledge and to honouring the spiritual dimension to life and she's maintained an interest in the various personal development workshops and events I have attended and facilitated. She knows the truth of Mooji's words that her healing lies in her own heart. I don't say it but I know that to encompass a belief in Eternal Life is to accept that Life continues beyond our physical form. In this moment it is enough for me to know this, I cannot contemplate death of the body. It is her heart that will guide all of us who are here to play our part in supporting her. I am reminded of the quote on the wall of the cardiology department of the hospital: 'A merry heart does good like a medicine, but a broken spirit dries the bones.'

We stay with Keso until 10 pm. I brush her hair for her; it is very matted and has taken over the pillow, making her uncomfortably hot. She asks for two plaits. Normally this would be an easy task but with the lump very close to the centre of her head, a middle parting would go right through it. I decide to take a detour. It is impossible to avoid the lump; my fingers brush against it – it is soft and hot and moves under my touch. I am nervous and exhausted; I only stepped off the plane a few hours ago, having been on a mental, emotional and physical roller coaster since seeing Keso on FaceTime. I don't even have the right tools for the job; Jess is making a list of the things she needs to bring next trip. We find a comb and I set about trying to make my daughter feel more comfortable. However hard I try not to hurt her, I know that I am. She winces, gasps and groans throughout the ordeal but tells me to keep going; 'It's OK, Mumma, it's not that bad,' she says. These are words we are to hear over and over again in the course of the next three months.

The job is finally done and I am left holding a handful of hair, most of which came away from on and around the lump. Keso is left with a small monk's tonsure, but she is happy with the outcome and feels more comfortable. We order her a light meal from the hospital's vegetarian restaurant; she hasn't eaten for some time and is beginning to feel hungry. I take this as a sign that although it is early days, she is slowly settling into recovery mode.

The nurse arrives to give Keso her medication. I learn that Dr Kay, the consultant neurologist, has visited, examined her and sent her for an MRI scan, the results of which reveal that our daughter has suffered a cerebral venous thrombosis (CVT), a rare and potentially devastating type of stroke. I read later that it tends to occur in young adults, especially women. The treatment for CVT is anticoagulant medication. Dr Kay was very quick in reaching his diagnosis and so when I arrive treatment has already begun. He has also prescribed a blood thinner to help remove the clot.

Before we leave for the night Jess and I give Keso a bed bath, wiping her down with baby wipes and sprinkling her with talcum powder. She is acutely aware that she is sweating heavily; she still has a fever, even though the air conditioning in her room is quite high, and she doesn't want to be 'offensively smelly'. This is also the beginning of the wonderful white support stocking, which she has to wear as a precaution against thrombosis after her stroke, particularly as she has very restricted mobility. The stocking is extremely tight and fits from toe to crotch and it becomes my job to take it off and put it on every day at shower time. I am exhausted; it's 10 pm, I have to go. I kiss and hug and stroke Keso and promise to be back in the morning.

Edward and Jess also live in Wan Chai, about a ten-minute walk from Keso. Jess offers me a bed for the night in their spare room. I accept gratefully, I don't want to be on my own in a strange apartment not knowing where anything is.

It feels like my head has hardly hit the pillow when Jess is shaking me awake. 'It's the hospital, Joan, they've called to say that Keso is having another seizure, I've told them we'll be there in fifteen minutes.' It's early in the morning and I scramble out of bed frantically pulling clothes and wash bag from my suitcase, and head to the bathroom. In no time at all I am dressed, drinking a cup of green tea and hastily eating a biscuit. I suddenly remember Jess's words: another seizure! Jess and I explode from the building and she runs into the main road waving at a passing cab.

When we arrive Keso is just coming round from the last seizure. She is dazed and disorientated and her speech is slow and slurred. She is very tired, she says, but wants to know what happened. She knows that she has been having seizures (a sudden surge of electrical activity in the brain) throughout the night, and that Dr Kay has been told. I keep talking to her as she is coming round trying to reassure her, I don't know what else to do.

As we are talking Keso suddenly says, 'Oh, Mumma, something's happening again, I can feel my leg going again, I can't control it!' I look on horrified as Keso slides into another seizure. Her body arches and twists and shakes uncontrollably, her face contorts, her mouth stretches wide and her eyes roll and then take on a fixed, glassy stare. This is my worst nightmare.

We call the nurses as soon as Keso alerts us and immediately two of them appear and call for more support. There are now five nurses around Keso, putting her flat on her side and gently holding her so that she doesn't injure herself. Jess and I cling to each other, eyes wide with fright. I am unable to look at the writhing body in front of me on the bed. Suddenly the nurses become aware of us and tell us to wait outside.

We sit on a gurney in the corridor, arms around each other, and watch nurses busily come and go between her room and the nurses' station. The hospital is built in the round with the nurses' station the hub at the centre, and the rooms, wedges that radiate out like the spokes on a bicycle wheel. No one speaks to us for a while until one of the nurses catches sight of us and our frightened expressions, and comes over to tell us that she knows it is very distressing to witness a seizure, but that Keso is in good hands and Dr Kay has prescribed anti-seizure medication which has just been administered. Later we are told that Keso will need to be on this medication for about a year, that she must not drink alcohol and that she won't be allowed to drive for at least two years. They move Keso to the Intensive Care Unit while she is still having the seizure so that they can monitor her more closely. Her heart rate and blood pressure are low. A phlebotomist arrives and fills several vials with her blood. She has pneumonia and a blood infection – the result of stomach acid entering her lungs during the seizures. They put her on intravenous antibiotics to combat the infections.

Dr Kay has arrived; I leave Keso in Jess's care and go out to the nurses' station to introduce myself. He tells me that Keso has had a stroke, is on medication and should make a full recovery in time, given her age and general level of fitness. He reassures me about the seizures, saying that the anti-epilepsy medication should deal with them. Later I am told by Keso that Dr Kay thought that she might be exaggerating some of the symptoms as they were so atypical: the fact that the paralysis was coming and going at first, that her speech was not affected, and that she was clearly fully conscious. The lump on her head and the terrible head pain were also a confusing set of symptoms, so that briefly he had a few doubts. This wretched lump!

The anticoagulant to help remove the clot is injected directly into her stomach twice a day. It is likely that they are responsible for causing the seizures as the clot moved and affected her brain.

Keso writes:
The injections in my stomach are really painful. As the needle goes in it feels like a normal injection, a quick, sharp pain, but then the pain continues and feels really sore. I ask for them to try my thighs instead; it is still really painful but slightly better.

It appears that the answer to pain, in the first instance, is more pain.

Dr Kay asks about Anthony and whether he will be able to come. I ask if he would mind speaking to Anthony when we FaceTime him and he is agreeable to this. Over the Internet he explains what has happened to Keso and her treatment, and Anthony asks if he thinks there should be a second opinion. There is a moment's awkward silence before Dr Kay says firmly that this isn't necessary. After Dr Kay has left Anthony asks me the same question and I agree with Dr Kay. Both Keso and I have confidence in him and like his manner. He is approachable, communicative, cautiously optimistic and accessible; these are not adjectives that I have had cause to use so freely in my dealings with the medical profession to date. Crucially, his diagnosis was swift, allowing for no delay in getting Keso onto the medication and the road to recovery. Anthony is reassured; I know that being so far away is frustrating and he wants to play his part in supporting Keso.

Keso's seizures:

I can tell they are about to happen, but in the seconds it takes for me to realise this and act, the seizure starts and it's too late for me to do anything. My body seizes and goes rigid, my arms and wrists stick out at strange angles, and then I start to shake. I'm aware of this for probably a second or so – just enough time for my brain to register I'm having a seizure – and then I black out. I'm not afraid going into them, just frustrated that I know I won't get to the bell in time to call for help. I remember being conscious for parts of the very long seizure. I remember nurses calling for more help, holding me in position, Dr Kay's voice, being rushed to the CT scanner. But after that it goes black. It's a similar feeling to fainting, I slip into warm, comfortable darkness and wake up groggy and exhausted, almost wishing I was still in the blackness. Another way I'd describe it is that strangely, seizing feels like the natural state. Like my body has been building up to this or needs to release this pent up energy, and the seizure is the way of making this happen. Like I've said, it never feels scary or confusing but rather almost natural, comforting, everyone else around me is much more afraid of it than I am.

Some people have what are known as auras with a seizure. That is a particular sensation just before they have a seizure. I don't think I had what you'd call a traditional aura – seeing a light, hearing a noise or being confused. But when they first put me on the blood thinners I remember lying in bed and suddenly feeling the nerves in my body as if they were being plucked like guitar strings. The sensation ran from my head down my spine and through my legs. It felt like someone was pulling on individual nerves, twanging them.

With an open mind, I read accounts of other experiences of seizures in an attempt to understand what my daughter is going through. Like Keso, some of them also use the words 'natural' and 'comforting'. The Russian novelist Dostoyevsky describes his seizures as blissful:

> A happiness unthinkable in the normal state and unimaginable for anyone who hasn't experienced it... I am in perfect harmony with myself and the entire universe.

While this might not be everyone's experience, I am reassured by his words.

Jay arrives in Hong Kong on February 5th to find Keso in the Intensive Care Unit. It is an emotional reunion.

Jay's story:
I should be happy right now; I should be bursting with excitement. Instead I'm sat in transit at Doha International Airport, exhausted physically, mentally and emotionally. I reflect on the events that have led to this moment...

It's November 17th 2013 and Keso and I have just passed through Heathrow to arrive safely back in London. We have been exploring the idea of living abroad for some time, and this ten-day trip to Jess and Edward has sold us on a new life in Hong Kong. At New Year we host our annual party and feature a Resolutions Board – Keso writes on it 'move to Hong Kong'.

It's June 2014 and we've moved in with my parents rather than renew the lease on our flat. Work has been taxing for both of us; we are really motivated about moving to Hong Kong…

It's August and Hong Kong feels like a pipe dream. We book a holiday, Christmas in the Philippines and New Year in Hong Kong. This way we can meet potential recruiters and employers face to face. Keso's been sending out her CV and following up on likely leads, and in November she receives a job offer! She's to start on January 9th; this transforms the nature of our holiday entirely, we'll need to find accommodation for a start. I haven't got a job offer but we decide to throw caution to the wind and make the decision to both just go! I submit my resignation at work, but unfortunately timings mean that I will have to fly back to the UK on January 11th to finish work.

It's December 23rd and the first leg of our move. Boxes have been packed and shipped, goodbyes have been said. We are at the airport with Keso's parents. I will be seeing them again but for Keso, Joan and Anthony this is their adieu. It makes me think about how I will cope when I'm in this position with my parents a few weeks from now.

On January 11th Keso comes to see me off at Hong Kong International Airport. We never knew when we booked this trip that it would be such a turning point in our lives. It's going to be a few difficult weeks, but I'm looking forward to what the future holds! At the end of January I book to return to Hong Kong on Friday, February 6th. Keso is planning to take the day off work to meet me at the airport and the following Monday is her birthday, so we can have a long weekend together. What she doesn't know is that I am actually planning to arrive on the Thursday and surprise her! I'm normally pretty bad at romantic gestures, so I'm quietly pleased with how I've managed to plan this, though in truth it was Jess's idea. Keso went home from work ill today. I hope she recovers in time; I'll be in Hong Kong in just over a week!

I check in on Keso regularly, she's still ill and if anything getting worse. I'm glad she's got Jess and Edward. I don't actually remember being told that Keso had been taken into hospital. All I remember is speaking to her earlier in the day – Saturday morning Hong Kong time – and her saying that she felt better and was going to get ready to go shopping with Jess. I'm on my way home when I notice a missed call from Anthony, who I call back immediately. Anthony and Joan share some shocking news with me and tell me that Joan is going to fly out to be with Keso as soon as possible. I call Jess and remember speaking to her for a long time; she's at the hospital with Keso. I remember that Keso didn't seem coherent, a lot of groans and laboured breathing, but she didn't seem panicked. I just want to be there!

I've cancelled my last few engagements in London and spent the last few days staying in touch with Keso and Jess. Joan is now in Hong Kong too. I take the last full day in London for myself, go to some of our favourite places, and prepare for when I arrive in Hong Kong.

It's February 4th, the day I fly. I know where I'm going but not what I'll find when I get there. Anthony visits and gives me a letter for Keso. He's also taken the decision to fly to Hong Kong as soon as he can. My parents take me to the airport; it's been a difficult time for them too. I can see the anguish in my mum's eyes even though she won't say anything. We embrace and I remind my parents of how much I love them and how amazing they've been.

And so here I am in transit in Doha International Airport, exhausted. When my flight is called I collect my things and prepare to board with a renewed sense of purpose that carries me through the fatigue. I know that when I arrive in Hong Kong everything that we planned will be irrelevant. The life we imagined will be on hold. I have a new plan now, and that is to be there for Keso. For now an emotional reunion awaits…

5 – SLOWLY SURFACING

Dive down deep into waters yet unknown
Journey with the spirit to the Soul
Collect the fragments from their watery grave
Reassembled surface soar...

Reflections:
I sit in the Silence, aware of the rhythm of my breathing. So much has happened in the past few days.

I do not recognise myself
In the mirror the face is familiar
But inside something has changed
I hear myself speak
See myself laugh, frown, smile
But I am not the same...

Tonight I can add weep to the list. I am trying to write an affirmative prayer, a 'Spiritual Mind Treatment' for Keso. Over the past few years I have come to understand that true prayer is never addressed to something separate and outside of ourselves, there is not God / Infinite Intelligence / Creative Force and me, but rather God/Source as me. A Treatment seeks to realign us with this truth. If we believe that the Creative Force is a force for good, and that we live in a benevolent universe, then it will reflect back to us that benevolence. A Treatment therefore affirms an acceptance of this Universal Creative Energy with which we interact through our thoughts and beliefs. This is where faith must triumph over fear and the 'conditioned mind'. Do I believe firmly without any doubt that the outcome I desire will be achieved? I am learning that it is one thing to nod my head sagely at this teaching in a classroom, and quite another to surrender my daughter's life and well-being to it as she lies ill in hospital. As Ernest Holmes writes, 'The one who wishes to demonstrate some particular good must become conscious of this particular good, if he wishes to experience it. He must make his mind receptive to it and he must do this consciously.'

I cannot do it on my own; I am in need of a faith lift. I contact Lynne, my metaphysics teacher. I write:

> Dear Lynne, I am with Keso in Hong Kong. She is in hospital having had a stroke with a blood clot on her brain. She has severe head pains and temporary paralysis of her left arm and leg. I am with her from 9 am to 9 pm, then fall into bed exhausted ready to start again the next day. I am attempting to write a Treatment to support the truth of her situation but I am tired and attending to her day-to-day needs, so would be grateful for any support you can offer us.

Lynne replies:

> This is just an acknowledgement of your email as I have just opened it. I will certainly contemplate the content and send a treatment ASAP. I was shocked to hear the news about young Keso and realise how hard this must be for you. At this stage, right now, I just want you to know that I am with you and the battle is not yours.

The battle is not mine – a great peace descends on me on reading these words. So often I have found it almost impossible to know where I stop and my daughters begin; it's as if we bleed into each other and I live what I imagine to be their pain. However she means it, Lynne's timely observation has helped me make the separation and enabled me to look after my needs so that I can support Keso to look after hers. To be truly effective is to live from the knowledge that we are all individualisations of the One Spirit, while establishing and observing the psychological and physical boundaries between individualised self and other, especially when the other is my daughter.

Lynne writes:

> *Here is a treatment that is for you and Keso. As ever please change the wording to suit if something doesn't feel right and of course the whole thing can be spoken in the first person or the third. But if you are speaking it for her, I have written it in a way that is for you both. After speaking the Treatment just rest for a couple of minutes in the Silence. Make sure you look after yourself too.*
>
> ### *Treatment for Keso*
> *I know that in my Deepest Self I am Eternally united with an Infinite Healing Presence, for there is a place deep within me where I am wide open to the Infinite. This place is the Secret Place of the Most High. In this Deepest Self I have never been ill, defeated, confused or unhappy. Here not a sound from the outer world can penetrate. Here Spirit with Spirit can meet. Here I sense my Oneness with that Eternal Peace which passeth understanding.*
>
> *Here I recognise that in Keso is that which is Greater than anything that can ever come against her. I do not try to conquer my fears by fighting them, nor do I run away from them. I simply occupy my thought with the quiet assurance that the will of God in Keso is Health and Wholeness.*

Infinite Spirit does not change even when my feelings about it change. My feelings come and go but the Peace is Eternal and Changeless. At my unhappiest moments Keso is just as much in the Healing Presence as at my highest peak. In my darkest hour, I am still in the Eternal Light. I accept this as the Truth regardless of my feelings.

I know that Infinite Intelligence is in every organ, cell and atom of Keso's body, operating and sustaining her body in perfect right action. This Healing Power flows through the medical profession and in every hand that touches Keso's body. She attracts only highly evolved individuals on her pathway. Her presence helps to bring out the spiritual, healing qualities in each practitioner. Doctors and nurses are amazed at her ability to heal and enjoy working as a healing team with her.

I know and affirm that her body is a safe place to live. The river of Universal Light washes clean anything unlike Itself making the crooked places straight and the rough places smooth. Keso is radiant, vital and alive! All is well.

And so it is.

I read the treatment and weep.

Anger past and present

Holding on to anger is like grasping a hot coal with the intent of throwing it at someone else. You are the one who gets burned.
Buddha

I have never been good at expressing anger. As a child I had seen enough of its destructive expression within my extended family and 1950s post-war London, and made the decision (albeit unconscious) to turn my back on it. What I failed to understand as a child was that anger will have its way with you. Detesting suppression, it will find ways to push to the surface and escape in any form it can. Through volcanic expression, withholding, mean behaviour in relationships, violence, poverty, disease, self-sabotage, guilt and addictions. This childhood decision on my part to ignore or swallow it, coupled with my childhood belief that my task was to bring peace and harmony within the family and wider society, resulted in a child overwhelmed by feeling responsible for the volatile expressions of others, and unable to acknowledge her own. Always ready to deny them, to suppress them and to insist that everything was all right. In this current stressful and uncertain situation how do I know if those early 'survival' beliefs and behaviours are trying to re-establish themselves, or if, as I believe, I have found a more assertive and healthy way to deal with this powerful emotion?

I know that I do not want to get 'burned' any more and so I have learnt to acknowledge and accept the feelings, thoughts and sensations in my body associated with anger, and observe them come and go without trying to suppress them. This combination of awareness and detachment helps bring me back to a place of calmness and clarity, from which I can act more effectively – more often than not. I remember vividly one moment of real anger, when Keso was in intensive care and in a great deal of pain and discomfort. The nurse responsible for Keso's care through this particular night demonstrated a lack of compassion and empathy. Instead of showing a willingness to be understanding and flexible about Keso's requests to be repositioned in the bed and to have her painkiller slightly earlier than had been agreed, as all the other nurses had, her response was inflexible and unsympathetic. Despite the fact that it added to Keso's distress and discomfort. In the past I would either have swallowed my anger and found ways to convince myself that she was acting in Keso's best interest, or become as rigid and fixed in my behaviour and expectations in defence of my daughter. Neither of which would have addressed Keso's needs. Instead I made it clear that I was here to support my daughter and make sure that she was comfortable, and that I would stay at her side to make sure that this was accomplished.

We did not see this nurse again, and those who looked after Keso continued to be kind, compassionate and responsive to her needs.

In the words of Thich Nhat Hanh, 'I would not (now) look upon anger as something foreign to me that I have to fight... I have to deal with my anger with care, with love, with tenderness, with nonviolence.' I have also been listening to Satish Kumar on YouTube, a former Jain monk, and long-term peace and environmental activist. He suggests that it is our desire to control that often leads us to violent actions and words. We need to cultivate nonviolence of the mind, and from this will flow nonviolence of speech. I cannot be certain that this idea was operating consciously in my interaction with the nurse, but something of the truth of these ideas must have informed how I dealt with the situation. My personal belief in a benevolent universe and the eternal goodness, loving kindness and givingness of Infinite Intelligence, is the most powerful antidote to anger that I know. And remember, this is a sacred journey – we are headed to the Light...

They have moved Keso to ICU and I am with her every day. I arrive early and stay as late as I can. Whenever it is possible I sleep in a chair next to her bed. She must know if she needs anything that I am here. I am getting a cold; it must be the air conditioning. Air conditioning is the curse of Hong Kong! Guidebooks warn you of the city's addiction to it, and for good reason. Unfortunately I didn't read any tourist material before catching my flight to Hong Kong and so I am unprepared for the frigid temperatures that greet me anytime I enter any building. I am told by Jess that workers keep a coat at work, which they put on when they arrive! The hospital is no exception. Perhaps it is a response to the devastating outbreak of Sars in Hong Kong around ten years ago, the deadly respiratory disease that killed over 200 people. Certainly Hong Kongers are very conscientious about public health and hygiene. Surgical masks are on offer as you step through the hospital door, individuals wear them on buses and in public spaces, to protect themselves and others. Certainly sneezing or coughing on a bus immediately attracts disapproving looks. Apartment blocks and office blocks take pride in letting you know how many times a day lift buttons, hand rails, door knobs and other public surfaces, are sanitised. I read that kindergartens require parents to record their child's body temperature in a special notebook each morning. I start to leave a heavy cardigan on the chair beside Keso's bed.

Everyone in the hospital is caring and compassionate, from the greeter at the door – who opens the door of taxis dropping people off and picking them up – to the consultants who visit Keso regularly. I am still finding my feet in this new culture of private healthcare. I am allowed and expected to do as much for Keso as I want, no one mentions visiting hours. In fact when Keso returns to the general ward after her seizures, I am asked if I could stay with her through the night. There are no other patients in the room, and I make myself comfortable in an armchair beside the bed, ready and waiting should she need anything. I move into Keso and Jay's apartment when Jay arrives, but spend very little time there apart from asleep. The fridge and cupboards are almost bare. I don't have time for breakfast, choosing sleep over food. At lunchtime I eat when Keso eats, and in the evening it's comfort food. But everything for me is on the run, fast, in between attending to Keso's needs in the hospital, anticipating what might be needed next day, shopping for healthy titbits for her, and writing the daily updates.

I am exhausted, in shock and fearful. Although I am supported by Jess, Jay and Edward in so many ways, I feel spiritually alone. To help Keso my faith must be strong and unshakeable, as part of my work is to remind Keso of hers. St Paul says that 'Faith is the assured expectation of things hoped for' and I agree with him. Faith, as we know, can move mountains. Lynne has been my salvation, I am moved and restored each time I read the Treatment and I read it often, committing parts of it to memory. There is a saying in 'New Thought' circles, 'Treat and move your feet'. I'm on my way!

Since my arrival I have been emailing friends and family to let them know about Keso. I write:

> I'm in Hong Kong with Keso. It's all been a bit dramatic. She was admitted to hospital on Friday with severe head pains and numbness on the left side of her body. Finally diagnosed as a blood clot on the brain. They are giving her an anti-coagulant and she is slowly improving. The paralysis is temporary and they say it will slowly go.

And then:

> Keso is in hospital. She had a stroke (cerebral venous thrombosis) a blood clot on the brain. She is having severe head pains and her left arm and leg are temporarily paralysed. She is being treated with an anti-coagulant and antibiotics and the consultant is optimistic about her recovery but it will take time.

Over and over I repeat these words to shocked friends and family; I post on Facebook and text people from my phone. It is a difficult job because it is all being done on my iPhone with two fingers. It is slow and painstaking work but the repetition begins to ground me. Finally I feel the numbness leave me. I am here in Hong Kong with Keso who needs me; there is work to be done.

With Lynne's help my faith is being restored. I send another email:

> Dear friends, I am here in Hong Kong with Keso who was admitted to hospital on Friday with severe head pains and loss of movement on her left side. She has since had an MRI scan and it turns out to be a blood clot on her brain (finally I can say her brain). She is taking an anticoagulant and we are told that she will gradually

recover the use of her left arm and leg. Could you all send healing please!

I send this email to the 'healing group'. We are a group of friends who have been meeting monthly for about twenty years – and came together as newly qualified therapeutic healers eager to talk about and practise our developing skills and experience in energy work. The group is my spiritual rock, the place I go to for this kind of support when my world falls apart. They all come back to me the same day:

> **Vanessa:** *Dearest Joan, I am holding Keso and you in my thoughts. I am sending out prayers and wish her the best for a swift recovery. My love and all my healing thoughts to you and all your family at this hard time...*

> **Nigel:** *Dear Joan, much concerned to read your news. I will of course send distant healing to Keso on a daily basis and greatly hope that she makes a speedy recovery...*

> **Jackie:** *How frightening for you all. Sending strong healing to you all. Glad you are there Joan...*

> **Maura:** *Oh dear Joan, what terrible news. I am praying and thinking and sending continuous healing thoughts to Keso and you. Praying for good outcomes, with love...*

> **Wendy:** *Oh Joan, so, so sorry to hear about Keso. You must be so worried, not to say scared, even though the prognosis sounds very positive. Thank goodness you are there with her, I'm sure it will help her recovery. I will definitely send healing to Keso and you and keep Anthony and Tunde in my thoughts. If there is anything I can do from this end do let me know.*

> **Barbara:** *Darling Joan, I am sending love and healing to you and dearest Keso and to all of you, her dear ones to whom she is beloved. And whatever moments of self-care you can find I wish you softness towards your own needs. I know Keso has faced challenge before with you alongside and she has unique strength. Much love to her,*

her dear partner, to Anthony and Tunde and your Mum.
And so much love for you dear Joan. Healing Light.

I knew they would not let me down! I am renewed by the words I read and the energy that comes with them. I bless them all. Barbara is referring to the operation that Keso had at the age of seven to remove a cyst from her tibia, and the extended time she spent encased in plaster from hip to toe.

Ernest Holmes, founder of The Science of Mind, writes:

> We must turn from all our worries, anxieties, and fears about our body and know that there is a normal pattern of health, an organising factor that knows what to do and how to do it, a perfect idea that exists and will express and manifest in us, as us, when we recognise it and accept it as doing so. The doctor can assist the body mechanically through surgery and medication; we can assist by the way we think and act.

I send and receive emails, focusing on the facts, as I know them, the positives in Keso's situation and our need for love and healing energy. When we receive the rare email or post that speaks of fear I gently remind them of our need to stay positive, keep strong, receive love:

> *Please don't worry or become negative, what Keso needs*
> *is everyone to bombard her with love. Every time fear or*
> *anxiety or worry threaten to overwhelm you please don't*
> *let them linger, just replace them with all the love you*
> *have for Keso.*

Messages of love and positivity come to us from around the world:

Louis: *Love and healing power to you all*

Camilla: *Love and strength to you both*

Bruce & Angela: *She will get better... she's far too stubborn not to*

Mana: Pensées positives pour vous!

Carrie: Brave young lady! Such grit and determination; God bless you!

Sheena: Sometimes the smallest steps are actually giant leaps! All very positive!

Beth: Love, hugs, thoughts, healing and more

Jonathan: Adding to the good vibes! Praying you'll be much better soon, sweet coz.

Clothilde: All the sweetness, all the smiles, all the warmth around her!

Martha: Yeah! Love Power!!! Xxxxxxxxxxxxxxxxxxxxxx

Reflections:

I sit in the Silence listening to my breathing. There is much talk of fighting and battles and beating things, and I don't like it. I don't challenge anyone when they use these terms but inwardly I feel that I have to do something to balance them out. Sometimes I silently recite an affirmation: 'There is peace in Keso's mind, body and spirit, the Peace of the World that passeth all understanding overcomes everything unlike Itself.'

Sometimes I leave the room or stop reading the message. But these words don't go away. Why don't I like them? I sit in the Silence... There is enough pain and disruption in Keso's life at the moment to make her feel vulnerable and helpless, she no longer feels in control of what is going on in her body, it is an anxious time. This is often the point at which people make the choice to believe that they are a victim, and start blaming others or themselves for the situation in which they find themselves. Whether the victim role is real or perceived, the anger and frustration that it generates are very real, and are a danger to their mental health. I am afraid that these messages of 'battles' and 'wars to be waged' will lead Keso down this self-destructive path. I relax into my breathing looking for an answer...

Although I have not read it in its entirety, I know of the Bhagavad-Gita, the sacred Hindu poem that I understand to be – among other things – an epic tale of the conflict between good and evil and a discourse on right action and duty. On the battlefield Lord Krishna tells his pupil Arjuna, 'plunge into the din of battle but keep your heart at the lotus feet of the Lord'. This is the quote that finds its way out of the Silence into my consciousness. I take it to mean that Life presents us with many 'battles' (I am discovering a positive energy in this word), which we should enter into with all our heart, without becoming attached to the outcome. Once we have made our choice for right action our responsibility is to stay open to a successful outcome. Keso has faith and a community of love, she has shown that she believes that she will get well – she accepts her role in the 'battle'. I am at peace with these words.

Anthony arrives on February 6th. The last email I receive from him says, 'love you, be patient, be positive'. It is good advice and it will be much easier to follow with him beside me.

Anthony's story:
Although I am at home, in one way it is OK because Joan is there and initially I am reassured. As the news gets worse I become frustrated, angry and sad. I move the photo of Keso and Jay into the kitchen, mainly to remind Doreen, my mother-in-law diagnosed with dementia, who Keso is, but it triggers great sadness in me each time I see it. I begin letting friends and family know about what has happened to Keso, telling them all how much she loves getting messages and suggesting that it would be best via Facebook. My brother-in-law Dave puts up a beautiful photo of Keso on Facebook, and writes:
> Sending big love and healing vibes to my beautiful
> niece, who is recovering from a serious illness in
> hospital in Hong Kong. If you can spare some good
> vibes please wish her a full recovery. She is lovely
> within and without...

Both of which move me to tears. My emotions come in waves; at one point I am sad and in tears, at another so angry I want to punch something – it's so unfair! It is good to make contact with Dr Kay on the iPad, but such brief contact doesn't really give me any real knowledge or understanding and Dr Kay is not definitive about the situation. I would like every avenue examined. However I feel that things are under control. The defining moment for me comes when Keso begins to have seizures and is admitted to the ICU. This is when it becomes serious and I am very worried, I just want to be there. I write to everyone:

> *The news is not good and very worrying. I spoke to Keso and she was OK but in some pain. Since then the pain has got much worse and she has had another two seizures. Joan was with her through all this but she has now been taken into intensive care. It's terrible and I feel desperate, I am seeing today if I can go out shortly.*

The following day I write:

> *The news is a bit better, after a night full of pain they have altered the drugs and they are now being given intravenously via her glucose drip. She has sat up, eaten a little and amazingly moved her left leg a little. Joan was with her all night and Jay is with her all day today. Cathay Pacific has come up trumps and I will be flying today. I will be with her on Saturday afternoon!*

Jay leaves for Hong Kong before me. The night before he leaves I have supper with him and his parents. Despite the numerous Why questions that we pose through out the evening both Jay and I are reasonably optimistic. I give Jay a letter for Keso; I think it is the first letter I have ever written her.

> *My darling Keso,*
> *I do love you so much. It is all so unfair why can't it be me an old man, I would give anything to swap places. BUT you are positive and determined and will get better and fully recover. It is all those traits of*

yours that I so admire that will get you through. BUT
be patient. You know via all your messages how
much you are loved. People from all over the world; I
had a long chat with Frede and Julie and also my ex-
wife Helen who also sends you loads of love. Is this
the first letter I have ever written you? It is great that
mum is there with you… Anyhow my love, all my
positive thoughts are sent to you with lots and lots of
love.

Two days later, leaving Doreen in Tunde's care, I leave for the airport feeling anxious but positive and relieved that I am on my way. Having said goodbye to my brother Bruce, who has driven me there, I sit down to have my coffee feeling upbeat because in thirteen hours I will be seeing Keso.

On my arrival in Hong Kong I am met by Jess. We chat away on the airport express as it speeds its way into Hong Kong Island. Jess brings me up to date and reading between the lines I understand that she is preparing me for my first sight of Keso. I am emotional but so relieved to see her and be with her that it is pleasure rather than pain that is triggered. I write:

I held Keso's left hand and she squeezed my hand.
What elation, it's amazing how such small things give
me utter joy! Dr Kay, a Hong Kong Chinese, is really
wonderful. He has a lovely relationship with Keso
and spends as much time as we need talking through
everything and anything. He is the most senior doctor
in his field, and until she begins to show good signs
of improvement he will see her twice a day, seven
days a week. He graduated at Cambridge, then went
to Guy's and had a brief spell at Lewisham hospital.

On February 8th Jay sends us the early morning email from Keso's bedside:

Heart was good nurses didn't raise any concerns. Blood
work came back in the night that showed a blood
infection, but her existing course of antibiotics is fighting

it, cough and fever pretty much down. In any case they won't do anything with the heart until they clear up the infection. They've taken some more blood this morning for tests. On the plus side, Dr Kay called last night and prescribed a steroid that relieved the intracranial pressure and the pain. It's starting to wear off now but we can ask Dr Kay about it again when he comes in. This really helped with her sleep; she went to bed saying she could feel it was going to be a good night. Definitely need to get some protein in her diet today, to get her energy levels up.

I have become familiar with the hospital, my second home for now. I spend many hours walking up and down flights of stairs on various errands, and particularly on my way to the canteen. In such sedentary times I relish every little bit of exercise I can get and rarely take the lift. At the top of each flight of stairs are photographs of beautiful natural scenes, and under each photograph a quote. They are a daily reminder to me to have faith and be grateful.

Uncountable blessings: 'He performs wonders that cannot be counted.'

God knows the way: 'The Lord will guide you continually, giving you water when you are dry and restoring your strength. You will be like a well-watered garden, like an ever flowing spring.'

Love never fails: 'Many waters cannot quench love, neither can the floods drown it.'

The gift of peace: 'I am leaving you with a gift – peace of mind and heart. And the peace I give is a gift the world cannot give. So don't be troubled or afraid.'

6 – ORDER OUT OF CHAOS

Give Thy blessing we pray Thee to our daily work
that we may do it in faith, and heartily

Thomas Arnold

It is February 9th, Keso's birthday, and she will celebrate it in the ICU, with both of us with her, just as she'd wished for before the unexpected happened.

Anthony writes:

> *Keso is very tired and has eaten very little despite gentle*
> *pressure from us. Every challenge is being thrown at her.*
> *In the last 24 hours her heart has stopped – once for 3.5*
> *seconds and twice for shorter periods. They are*
> *concerned and the cardiologist has been to see her. He is*
> *monitoring her heart and she might need a pacemaker*
> *temporarily, but Dr Kay like us, wants a minimum of*
> *interventions. He observes that the heart is simple and*
> *that his colleagues should try studying the brain, that's a*
> *real challenge!*

Keso's phone is weighed down with a ton of birthday messages. Anthony and I leave the hospital at 10 pm the night before and go shopping for something to give her. This is not your typical birthday celebration, but we find a tee-shirt on which is written 'Joy, Happiness, Luck, Prosperity, Peace'. We agree that this is both useful – Keso finds the hospital pyjamas too hot – and appropriate. We buy a birthday cake on the way to the hospital, and the hospital also presents her with a small one. Jess arrives with cupcakes as a thank-you for all the nurses on the ICU. One of her regular nurses greets Keso with positive determination, in the form of a local phrase – 'Add oil!'

Dr Kay, Keso's manager Emma, and her regional manager Andy are also with us for the celebration. They are friendly, concerned and supportive.

During her time in ICU Anthony, Jay and I have provided around-the-clock care, each of us sleeping in a chair next to her bed ready to get her whatever she needs. The nurses have had a bed made up for us in the visitors' room but we don't use it, we want to stay with her. We are told firmly that this is contrary to the rules in ICU, but they are compassionate and, having done their duty in telling us, they get on with their work and leave us alone. We are truly grateful. It has taken me a while to understand the culture of this Seventh Day Adventist-run private hospital, but I know she is in the right place when, on my first day there, stepping out of the taxi I read the sign: 'We pray that you may be in good health, and that it be well with your soul.'

Much later when I decide to read about the institution in which we have put our faith, I learn that Adventist promotes the philosophy of total health:

> This means that we would not be satisfied with the diagnosis and successful treatment of the patient's medical problems. We view every patient as a whole person in the total context of his beliefs, family, work, and life style, and seek to restore him to a full functional life.

We are experiencing this philosophy in action for ourselves.

Dr Fung, the cardiologist, visits. He introduces himself in what we now know to be the traditional manner – holding out his card to Anthony with two hands and a brief bow. We have learned that we are expected to take it with two hands and a brief bow, look at it for a few seconds and then put it away. But Anthony is distracted and fails to do this – just another ignorant foreigner, we imagine he thinks! After monitoring her heart for a few days Dr Fung gives Keso the all-clear. He is, we observe, somewhat appropriately for a cardiologist, rather a heartthrob among the nurses.

Reflections:

I sit in the Silence and think about all that has happened over the past few days. An attitude of gratitude, we are told, creates blessings and unlocks the fullness of life. I am full of gratitude for the love, support and treatment that Keso is receiving. I am focused on positive thoughts and the posts that I have suddenly been noticing on Facebook support me in this. I am grateful to Carl Jung and his concept of synchronicity: *meaningful* (spiritually collaborative*) coincidences*. Today Dr Christiane Northrup posts:

> *True health begins with your thoughts. Thinking about comfort, strength, flexibility and youthfulness attracts those qualities into your life and body. Dwelling on illness, fear, disease and pain does just the opposite. Your work is to notice and change your thoughts and move them in the direction of health and happiness.*

From out of the Silence it comes to me that there is more that can be done to support Keso's return to health. The doctors are all doing what they can; I am supporting Keso to stay positive and have faith; friends and family are sending love and healing. To further add to this holistic approach, I think about contacting my homeopath in London, but before I can do this I receive an email from a guardian angel in the guise of Julia:

Keso is constantly in my thoughts and prayers as are you and Anthony. You all will stay there for as long as you have need of them. I appreciate the update so much, thank you for your thoughtfulness when you have so much else going on. Please pass on my birthday wishes for blessings to Keso. I've sent them to her already by energetic carrier but a physical delivery is always a good bonus.

P.S. I don't know if you use homeopathy, but if you can get your hands on some Cocculus 30c, it might be very helpful for you and Anthony – its particularly good for when you are under a lot of stress and anxiety and long hours, losing sleep caring for a loved one who's ill...

This is the start of a correspondence at the heart of Keso's journey back to full health, and to my ability to manage my own needs in the days ahead. Julia generously shares her knowledge and experience with us but leaves it with us to decide what to use and when to consult with the doctors.

To Julia I write:

I will pass on your birthday wishes as soon as Keso wakes. Gratitude has to be expressed in return for all the love coming our way! Many thanks for the homeopathic advice – synchronicity – I was about to email my homeopath back home. I will find some Cocculus. This evening I made a video of Keso taking her first real meal in days, a beef burger! But who cares – I will try and send it to you – I never thought I'd be so happy to see her eat one!

Julia replies:

Too funny about the Cocculus! That was great synchronicity! And I can't tell you how much pleasure the video gave me... Keso's a star! What a wonderful indication of real progress! Bless the cow that provided the meal. And bless you for keeping me posted on Keso's status, I am truly grateful in return. With love and huge doses of strength and encouragement.

The next day I hear from Julia again:

such wonderfully good news from you yesterday about Keso's continued progress! Here are some thoughts for essential oil supplemental therapy specifically suggested for neurological function. Young Living has a wonderful reputation for purity of product and I've had great success with them. They've recently opened an office in Hong Kong and you should be able to find out through customer service where you can purchase the oils. Have a look and see if you think any of these suggestions might be helpful.

My personal experience with helichrysum used on a dog with a bruised lung after a car accident was it immediately brought oxygen saturation up from 38% to 92% and stabilized the heart rate. At first the vet thought the machine had broken, but he couldn't argue with the results. It also helps to dissolve blood clots.

Brain Power has some amazing testimonials from people who've experienced traumatic brain injuries/events but I've never personally used it for that—I just use it to keep me focused. And I use Purification for just about everything infection related—I always have a bottle with me when I visit the hospital. On top of stimulating the brain in general, Peppermint wakes you up when you're dragging, so you and Anthony might find it useful for that. A good inhale or two and a rub on the neck does the trick. (But you absolutely can't use it in conjunction with homeopathic medicines, it will antidote them.) All these oils can be applied neat except on babies.

Never under estimate the power of Silence! Around Keso there is now developing an integrated and holistic approach to her health and well-being.

Barbara contacts me:

Circle of Love
Dearest Joan, I know it's evening there and as I write this it's lunchtime here in Bournemouth. I wanted to let you know that a whole legion of healers are surrounding Keso with love and healing. And you and Anthony and all of you are right there in our hearts too. Also a bunch of us will be tuning in for Keso this evening and subsequent evenings at 9 pm for 10 minutes so we can be there together; Light and love dear friend.

I reply:

Bless you and all the other healers. I am with Keso in the ICU and will tune in too. May I ask you to include her cousin Naium, like Keso he has had 2 seizures today (epilepsy) and is in our local Lewisham hospital.

Delcia and other friends and colleagues from the Association of Therapeutic Healers (ATH), contact me:

Delcia: *Goodness Joan, I am sorry to hear about Keso. I will certainly send healing. I will ask other healers if they will be willing to do so too. We have an ATH Core Group meeting this afternoon, so I will ask if we can send healing from there together too; and healing for you too.*

Jen: *Dear Joan I am so sorry to hear of Keso's stroke and am sending love, light and healing to her and to you all. Stay strong, blessings.*

Linda: *My dear Joan, I'm sorry to hear from Del about Keso, I'm holding you in my thoughts and sending my love and healing.*

Barbara: *Dearest Joan, Keso and Anthony, there are lots of us all around you sending love. I send you a picture of Kwan Yin who is from where you are right now, of course. She is the one who 'hears the cries of the world', and symbolises mercy and compassion. She insisted in walking right into the 9 pm circle where I had lit the* *candles. Mine is one of many hearts sending a constant flow of love and healing for Keso and for Naium.*

I contact my friend Jacqui in the weaving workshop that I attend at Morley College, to let her know and am touched by the number of weavers who send us love and good wishes. I am asking the Universe for help and the Universe is responding. With each email I weep at their generosity of spirit. I know the metaphysical 'theory' of how the Universe operates, but to experience the Law in action is truly awesome and life-changing. Keso is so open to this approach; my requests to let others know and to share the day-to-day struggles and achievements are all greeted with a 'Yes, Mumma'. Our daily updates are all read by her first and she changes none of them. While I have been keeping her up to date with my efforts on her behalf, I am making a lot of the decisions myself. Her energy and attention are needed to overcome the more immediate health challenges. But as she slowly improves I feel it is time to hand the reins over to her.

I write to Julia:

Thank you so much for your thoughts on complimentary treatments for Keso. I contacted Young Living in Hong Kong; they are located in the same district in which Keso lives. I also forwarded your email to Keso, as she is at last able to make decisions for herself. She wants me to order Brain Power and Peppermint and I will also order Purification. Unfortunately Brain Power is only available through the U.S. outlets, but I think I can order it online; it's just a question of how long it will take to get here.

In the end it proves impossible to order it here in Hong Kong and so Julia offers to send it to us from Florida.

7 – FIRST STEPS

The journey of a thousand miles begins with a single step
Lao Tzu

Keso is back on the medical floor in her old three-bed room. Her roommates, both of whom are elderly women, arrive with their two Filipino carers and an iPad. Once they are settled in, one of the carers departs and the other one switches on and sets up the iPad. There are bags of food to store away. It is not long before a face appears on the screen, questions are asked and answered, and the elderly patient is spoken to and scrutinised. The doctor appears, bows to the screen, sits down and I imagine takes the enquirer on the screen through the diagnosis, treatment and update. Another bow and the doctor is on his way.

I am surprised by this use of the technology in healthcare, but it makes sense. The carers are caring, offering me smiles and assistance, and Keso encouragement and support. We have something in common, caring is hard work even when it's for someone you love so totally. This is her first night for a while with none of us there. We receive her morning email at 7 am: a rather sad Keso tells us of a sleepless night with nurses in and out, and lights going on and off as they deal with a distressed, elderly patient. Anthony is on early-morning duty and he soon transforms his daughter into a smiling, less anxious Keso. Dr Kay visits; blood test and scans are all cautiously good news. He would like Keso to write an article about her stroke for a medical journal, and is keen to know if she is up to the task. He is happy to hear from Anthony that writing is a major part of her professional role and something that she does very well.

We have settled into a routine: Anthony on breakfast duty, me on lunch duty, and Jay on the evening shift. Jess comes as often as she can, usually having undertaken some practical task on our behalf. She brings with her a lightness and humour that we all desperately need. She also brings much-needed girly talk for Keso; of shopping, nail parlours, the latest fashion – stories to make her laugh. She tantalises me with talk of all sorts of girly outings for us when Keso is better! Edward comes every evening after work, arriving around 7.30 pm, often with supper for Keso and news of his day. He is Keso's link to normality, bringing everyday tales of meetings, lunches, articles read, news heard, photos taken and his general observations on life. He never misses a night and always hits the spot with Keso. Often after sharing his day he will sit quietly on his mobile – a reassuring companion, ready to act when needed.

I have discovered the number 15 bus, which stops outside the hospital and can be caught around the corner from Jess and Edward, and it is now my preferred mode of transport. I enjoy my late morning walks to the bus stop, often stopping at Boulanger Eric Kayser to collect delicious elevenses for us. The bus makes me feel more 'normal'. Observing fellow travellers going about their daily lives allows me to be part of something reassuringly ordinary on my journey to the extraordinary that is now our daily experience. I also need the exercise; my day consists of a lot of sitting.

Anthony and I often leave together around 10.30 pm, exhausted, ready for a good night's sleep, but Jess and Edward stay on. Jay, her love and her rock, is the last to leave, although he sometimes stays the night if she is feeling particularly low. Usually we take the bus, but if we are very tired, a taxi. On a couple of starlit, balmy nights we walk – along the peaceful Bowen Trail, and the dazzling neon cityscape of Hong Kong lights our way home. Through the Hopewell building, entering at the 17th floor, we take the lift down and exit opposite Jess and Edward's road. I love the routes provided by the public right of access to buildings across the city. The Bowen Trail is the city's main jogging track. Originally a viaduct, the 4km trail snakes its way along the slopes of Victoria Peak, overlooking Hong Kong's concrete and glass skyline, but itself covered in lush, green vegetation. In the morning, incense sticks waft smoke at the small shrines to be found along the route, and elderly Hong Kongers can be found practising their Tai Chi along its route.

My main practical hospital duties are to give Keso her daily shower and comb her hair. Showering Keso is a strenuous activity. The tight white stocking has to be removed at the bedside, and then after giving her a helping hand into her wheelchair we're off to the bathroom. She cleans her teeth slowly with her left hand; then its pyjamas off and I carefully bag and tape the arm with the cannula, ready to take the medication, so that no water can get in. I settle her back in the wheelchair and position her in the shower cubicle.

Getting the temperature right takes a few moments but finally she gives a satisfied sigh as I aim the shower and gently hose her down. Once she's wet I soap her like a baby; the final rinse takes some time, as she loves the feel of the warm water on her skin. When she finally, reluctantly calls time, it's off with the water and on with the baby oil, liberally applied as Keso has very sensitive skin. Then I start to dry her, the weak arm first, taking all of its weight as I rub the towel along it. Next I dry the arm with the cannula – a gentle pat dry so as not to dislodge the needle and tubes. I dry her back – spreading another towel over the back of the chair so that she can lean back once dry. Legs next, her left leg weighs a ton, it's hard to hold it up and I have to remember to gently lower it to the ground once it's been dried. Finally she stands, pulling herself up on the towel rail, while I pat dry her bottom! We are transported back to Keso's childhood, both of us, I think, enjoying the intimacy that this brings.

I think about my time as a student with Petruska Clarkson. Described as 'one of the most significant figures in the history of Gestalt therapy in England', Petruska wrote a book on human relationships called *The Therapeutic Relationship* and described 'the 5 relationship model'. I think my time here with Keso reflects the 'reparative relationship' described in her book: 'a corrective, reparative, or replenishing relationship or action where the original parenting was deficient'. It is my opportunity to make up for past omissions.

Being self-employed and running a business, work claimed a great deal of my attention, often taking me to different parts of the country for days at a time. I struggled with the balance between self-fulfilment through work and through family. Like many other mums I experienced a mother's guilt at not being present at many of those landmark events in her school life and adolescent years, as her father was. I feel blessed to have this time with her.

It is strenuous work in a small space, which despite the air conditioning, gets hot and humid by the time we have finished. Back to bed, on with the tight white stocking, and then it's hair to be brushed and plaited with the least discomfort possible. I wash her hair only once in hospital, during her first shower, and I am daunted by this task. It is difficult to get it clean and avoid the lump but I do my best, washing the length of her hair quite vigorously but being very gentle with her scalp. I sit her on a chair beside her bed and spend at least an hour parting it into small two-inch sections, and then combing it out section by section before putting it into two plaits for her. We are all aware of the lump and its changing contours. When we raise the question with Dr Kay he seems to be uncertain about it. He is, however, keeping a daily, watchful eye, but says firmly first let's deal with the stroke and get Keso moving again, that's the priority. He is clearly confused by it but thinks maybe the pressure from the clot has pushed fluids up into the scalp. He thinks that treating the stroke will treat the lump; this is why he prefers to leave it alone at this time rather than risk further infection.

Anthony writes:

> Thank the Lord she has had a peaceful night. I think we are on the road to recovery, which will have many new challenges… Next task is to sort out the payments and the insurance reimbursement, as we have to pay for everything up front and claim it back. We are so lucky to have the NHS in the UK. Jay has been working hard on this. His love and support are so important. Keso is a lucky lady. I must remember to have that 'what are your intentions' conversation with him… Here is a message from Keso herself typed with her left hand!

> Thank you all so much for your support. I have read every single one of your messages and they have touched my soul. Being surrounded by such a network of love has made this all slightly easier to come to terms with and see a road to recovery. I love you all very much.

> …A lot achieved; a shower, standing, exercises and a trip outside! Maybe a bit too much as she is very exhausted, but proud of her achievements. There's a long way to go but a start has been made. Dr Kay is having a day off, his first since Keso came in 12 days ago. Tomorrow we will have a discussion with him about discharge and the future…

On February 14th – supported by the physiotherapist and a walking aid – Keso walks for the first time in 14 days! Anthony's update reads:

> Firstly please let me know if you would now like to opt out of the updates as things move forward if you are getting too much information. The news today is all about the walk. She walked the round of her floor three times today (see Facebook video). Amazing and real progress, Dr Kay is predicting that Keso will be able to go home on Tuesday 17th. Also for the first time she has had some pain free moments. Her appetite is good.

No one asks to opt out; indeed we receive several emails from people saying how much they look forward to their daily updates. Anthony writes:

> Firstly to repeat, your support has been absolutely extraordinary and helped us all. The network from New Zealand, Sweden, Australia, Kenya, America, Guyana, Ireland, France, Singapore, Mexico, Hong Kong, the Philippines, and of course little old England. Apologies to any country we have left out... Joan and I are having a quiet morning in Keso and Jay's flat. I love this flat it is so minimalist, no clutter and no weavings at every turn!! We will soon decorate it for Chinese New Year (18th). The usual early morning email from Keso was so encouraging. She had a good night's sleep and her wires and telemetry (for data collection) have been removed... We have come a long way since Keso gently squeezed my finger, just like a baby. Now it's a long walk along the corridor where the brainpower needed is the equivalent of that needed for working out the theory of relativity or devising a strategy to make Ed Miliband electable.

Jay goes to collect the wheelchair and the walking aid from Hong Kong Red Cross, which we've hired for one month. Keso writes:

> The least said about last night the better, so much pain, but it's over now and I get to go home soon! Hear mum

isn't coming at all today so just make sure you send a decent outfit with dad and I can't wait to see you at home later! Can point my left foot! No flexing yet, but progress! More Peppermint oil tomorrow!

Keso on pain:
The pain is constant – like something is trying to pull my head apart and acid is in my sinuses. I tell Jess before I go into hospital that I feel like I want to peel off my own scalp to relieve the pressure. The only way to survive is with painkillers but they always wear off before I can take the next dose. Night times are worse, I don't sleep properly until Dr Kay prescribes the steroids, which help with the pain a lot. The pain also makes my head feel like it is under constant pressure – I stretch my mouth wide and adjust my jaw to try and relieve the feeling. Being immobile makes my scalp sensitive and irritable. My plaits dig into my head and pull my hair and I want to adjust position but I can't find anything comfortable. Plus lying on my left side is pretty much impossible because of the paralysis – and lying on my right isn't much better as my limbs flop over to one side or sit uncomfortably... The pain is just constant and exhausting, worse on my right side. A constant burning pressure in my head that feels like it is forcing something through all the individual layers of my flesh...

I write to our friends Wally and Sandra:

What a roller coaster ride we've been on! A one in two million chance of getting this rare form of stroke. Keso has been amazing through paralysis, seizures, heart stoppages, chest infection, pneumonia, 'the lump', antibiotics, painkillers, anti-epilepsy medication, twice daily injections of anticoagulant into her stomach, and near constant excruciating pain. But look where she is now!

Keso leaves hospital on my birthday and the day before Anthony heads back to London. Jay writes:

discharged from Hong Kong Adventist Hospital with prescribed medication to treat bleeding profile, seizures, pain, stomach ulcers and intracranial pressure. The lump is still present.

We have a celebratory supper in their apartment with Jess and Edward – a delicious Asian fusion take away, washed down with homemade non-alcoholic cocktails and followed by my birthday cake! I am not expecting gifts – Keso's homecoming is the best present I could ever have – but Jess buys me a beautiful felted shawl; she knows how cold I've been in the hospital, has lent me hers and now presents me with one of my own. The celebration is rounded off with an energetic rendering of Stevie Wonder's 'Happy Birthday', recorded for our next update!

Anthony has booked us into a very nice hotel on the airport site and so after our meal and emotional farewells we leave Keso and Jay to their first ever night together in their new home, and set off for the airport. I am sad to say goodbye to Anthony; since his arrival he has played a vital role in all our lives. Sergeant major-like organising rotas; making shopping lists; creating order in the apartment – we have to buy a lot of equipment for the kitchen as Keso had only been in the apartment for a couple of weeks before her stroke. He has endeared himself to the concierges that cover the block twenty-four hours. We are well known at Fusion, the supermarket on the corner of Keso and Jay's road. The women who serve in the restaurant in the hospital always have a word of greeting for him. Whom will the doctors talk to now? After Keso he is their next port of call. We will all miss him. But his leaving is also a sign that Keso – now back in her own home – is on the road to recovery and for that I am overjoyed!

Reflections:
I sit in the Silence happy and at peace. I have read somewhere that part of true happiness involves being of service to others, and I am happier now than I have been for some time, in service to my

daughter. Even though I end each day exhausted and my body sore and stiff, there is amazingly a *peace that passes all understanding... guarding my heart and my mind.* To focus so completely on the needs of another must lead to a stepping away from the ego towards the realisation of the True Self. Wayne Dyer helps us to recognise the **ego** at work by referring to it as the way in which we '**e**dge **G**od **o**ut'. We think we know best and don't leave room for the miracles that happen in our lives every day if we 'let go and let God'...

This service has become a golden thread
Woven into the tapestry of my everyday
It shines into the darkness
And a flame is kindled in my heart
To burn away the dross

I live more fully the qualities of my own heart centre
Compassion healing unconditional love peace
Gifts to be experienced and expressed
Through service to others...

Lao-tzu speaks powerfully and eloquently of the consequence of living from the heart:

If there is radiance in the soul it will abound in the family
If there is radiance in the family it will be abundant in the community
If there is radiance in the community it will grow in the nation
If there is radiance in the nation the universe will flourish

I am happy and at peace because I also can now see the bigger picture.

8 – KUNG HEI FAT CHOY

May prosperity be with you!

The hotel is vast, filled with crew and passengers in transit from around the world. From our window we can almost touch the planes on the runway. But it is surprisingly quiet and very comfortable. In the morning, in the cathedral-like restaurant, breakfast is available to suit every cultural palate. We eat our fill – Anthony going for the full but eclectic breakfast – reflecting the 'league of nations' that surrounds us. Hong Kong airport is truly an international hub. I walk with Anthony to the departure gate, hugs and kisses are exchanged, and I stand waving him off until he disappears from sight.

I feel like a local now, I know my way around the airport and the journey back 'home' is very familiar if a bit flat. I watch the activity on Lantau Island as the airport express snakes its way to the mainland, wondering what the next few weeks will bring and thinking that it won't be long before I am making this trip myself with Keso and Jay waving me goodbye.

Anthony sends an update from London:

> *Well folks, I am back in London, typing this from my bed as I recover from a 13-hour flight and time muddles. Probably even more typos than usual and no Keso to 'tut tut'. This might be my last update as after this email I am handing over to Joan. So first some thanks: Julie thank you for the French translations and keeping France informed. George, thank you for keeping your clan informed. Hong Kong support team Jay, Jess and Edward you have been amazing. Thank you to those who have provided much needed financial support. Thank you for all the love and caring, it has been really important for Keso.*

We have managed to order the essential oils Purification and Peppermint, but have problems with Brain Power, which is not available in Hong Kong. We have taken up Julia's offer to send us her almost full bottle.

Keso's first outing in the wheelchair is to Arsenal Street. She's a 'Gooner', having supported Arsenal football club since she was put in her first Arsenal baby-grow twenty-six years ago. Her dad is delighted to see the photo of her and Jay under the street sign. Particularly as Jay supports Manchester United! We have a very tasty brunch at a nearby French bistro.

I am careful to give Keso and Jay some time alone every day, and so after breakfast each day I take myself off to explore the city. I discover the very local Wan Chai Market for groceries, fruit and vegetables, and within a ten-minute walk, Causeway Bay, described as 'a microcosm of the entire Hong Kong shopping scene with its luxury malls and mid-priced boutiques'. I also discover Jardine Crescent, a street market offering bargains galore. I shop in Uniqlo, Zara, Forever 21 and the stalls on Jardine Crescent, offering one-off samples at ridiculous prices. I do love a good shop! In my defence I do not have enough layers to deal with the changes in temperature between the outdoors, the air-conditioned hospital, and Keso and Jay's unheated but air-conditioned apartment. Perhaps my most exciting find is the equivalent of our UK pound shop – the $12 dollar shop on Hennessy Road. Keso's kitchen has been equipped courtesy of this Aladdin's cave. I have even found wool for my weaving here!

I do not confine myself to shopping. I have discovered a hidden, elevated park a stone's throw away near the harbour. There are beautiful sculptures, a waterfall and pond and shady areas where elderly women and men practise their Tai Chi in the morning. The early mornings in Hong Kong are fresh, with a gentle breeze; it is the time of day I love, and one in which to experience a moment of silence and calm before the Island wakes up and the streets get busy. Sometimes I walk to Victoria Park, a busy leisure space close to the shopping area of Causeway Bay, and sit and read my book. My favourite park is Hong Kong Park. It's a beautiful space with fountains, lakes where turtles bask, hothouse, café and traditional tearoom and tea museum. Part of the attraction for me is the novelty of accessing the park up through Central Shopping Plaza via escalator. Taking an escalator in a shopping complex and exiting into such a beautiful park has captured my imagination!

Keso is back home recovering and Anthony has returned to the UK. My thoughts turn to my own inevitable departure and how to continue to support Keso when I am no longer here with her. I decide to compile my own set of 'daily guides'. The local $12 shop has packs of small business-sized cards with pretty images on one side, and their own colourful envelopes. I begin writing statements that I hope will resonate with Keso and help her maintain a positive attitude. I have bought, from the same shop, a brightly coloured child's bag, in the form of a mini suitcase, in which to keep them. Whenever I have time on my own I add more to the bag. I plan to give her this when I am leaving together with a Mumma 'pep talk'.

It is February 19th and Chinese New Year is upon us. We have decorated the apartment with good luck and prosperity symbols. We have discovered a little family-run stationery shop not far from the apartment. The daughter speaks English and we take advantage of this to learn more about the meanings of the various symbols, decorations and Chinese phrases on sale. Before Anthony left he handed over the little red envelopes – *Lai See* – each containing a crisp new $20 note, to each concierge. These red packets are given from 'old to young', 'big to small' and 'senior to junior'. The colour red is regarded as the symbol of energy, happiness and good luck, and is offered as a blessing to the receiver. Anthony remembers to hand them over with both hands, a bow, and 'kung hei fat choy' (happy new year).

Jay, Keso and I head for Tamar Park on the seafront to watch the Chinese New Year firework display. It takes us about half an hour to negotiate the route, with Jay pushing the wheelchair along pavements and elevated walkways, waiting for elevators to take us up and down the various levels. We meet with Jess, Edward and friends, and watch an amazing light display with fireworks from across the water in Kowloon; everyone is taking photos, and everyone is incredibly well behaved, and there is no litter to be seen anywhere. This is certainly not like Trafalgar Square on New Year's Eve! Keso is well wrapped up with woolly hat and scarf but is still hunched against the cold, looking pale and tired. I am anxious to get her back home.

Keso is a stylish young woman – ask anyone. At the age of twelve she was having *Vogue* magazine delivered to our door every month. She is skilled at applying her make-up; her wardrobe is impressive; she has boxes of shoes, beautiful handbags and accessories to compliment it all. Out of hospital, our stylish daughter has disappeared into black leggings, tee-shirts, sweatshirts and baggy sweaters. Illness strips you of your identity and your enthusiasm for everything but your recovery.

I write:

> *Kung hei fat choy from Tamar Park! Buildings lit up and amazing fireworks. A late night for us and for Keso, who is having a difficult time adjusting to being home. I guess she's feeling the pressure of managing her own recovery now, but she's not alone. The lump appears to be spreading to other areas and is causing swelling around her eye, adding to her low mood. That wretched lump again! However she has settled into a routine with her exercises, which we have supplemented with exercises from ARNI, the Institute for Stroke Rehabilitation, back in the UK. Thank you John Teasdale for the introduction. Her first appointment with Dr Kay since being discharged is next week and we are all keen to hear what he has to say about the lump, although he says himself that the rarity of the stroke means he has to wait and see. I am happy with his 'when-in-doubt-wait-and-see' approach.*

Keso's mood has changed, she believes her movement – rather than improving – is becoming more and more erratic and difficult to control. She see-saws between quiet and sullen, and angry and explosive, and appears to be on the verge of giving up. 'What's happening to me? All this effort – what's it for when I'm going backwards!' I try to reassure her. 'You've been pushing yourself too hard, Keso,' I tell her. 'Don't forget you've had a very serious stroke, there are bound to be moments like this when things aren't moving forward as quickly as you'd like them to. Perhaps you should rest a little. Please don't despair; all of this negative thinking will affect your energy levels. Look at how much you have achieved. Our appointment with Dr Kay is next week, let's wait and hear what he has to say.'

Despite the exercise regime, Keso feels that she is not improving. There are tears of frustration and anger when her control of her left foot begins to deteriorate, and her hand–eye coordination exercises become more difficult. She withdraws, becomes quieter and more listless. I lavish her with love, try to distract her, tell her that she has been doing so much that she is probably just tired. Once Keso has a plan she can be determined and unstoppable; perhaps she has just over-extended herself and needs to rest a little. Her confidence in herself is really being affected.

From his bed back in London, Anthony emails Keso:

> Yo! My darling, its quite odd writing this while you are asleep; and you will be writing one to me while I am asleep. Miss you a lot and spend a lot of time sending you positive vibes. I know you will fully recover given your determination; patience is the hardest thing. I am writing this waiting for Match of the Day. Say it quietly; we have just gone above Manchester United... Oops guess what, I fell asleep... awake again. One question for you and Mum – Mum's birthday meal and cake, I think there was an understanding that we would pay for it? Looking forward to Skyping you tomorrow morning...

Keso replies:

> Missing you lots too. I know I'll get through this too, determined to be even stronger afterwards, it's just some days are easier than others...

I email Karen, my coach and now my friend, back in the UK:

> Keso is worrying a bit about work and the cost of all this treatment. She has insurance but we have had to pay for it all up front and wait to be reimbursed. However I am remarkably well! Assailed by very few negative thoughts and able to observe those that sometimes arise, with more and more detachment. Life is good and I am able to live as that still, peaceful, spacious place within, more and more!

Reflections:

I sit in the Silence and I am grateful. I have allowed fear and scarcity their expression, but not fallen into the trap of attaching myself to them. They are just thoughts that come and go and I am doing my best not to feed them. Instead my attention is focused on abundance, I am cultivating an attitude of gratitude and in doing so the universe is drawing to me more and more to be grateful for. I am learning first hand the power that can be released through the words 'thank you'. I am writing a gratitude list at night, before I go to bed, of all the good things – however small and trivial – that have occurred during the day. In this way the blessings of the day are my last thoughts before I fall asleep. It stands to reason that what I plant in my subconscious mind will germinate and grow in my life. This regular expression of gratitude is – I know – retraining my mind away from negative thinking and towards love and appreciation. I know that I attract into my life what I focus on in my thinking and so I am exercising some care over what I allow to linger in my mind. There is a growing body of scientific work that shows that kindness and gratitude are traits that lead to higher levels of well-being, and that people who practice gratitude on a regular basis have stronger immune systems. Given Keso's current situation, this adds to my resolve to circulate gratitude. I discover I am in good company in my attitude to gratitude:

> **Plato:** a grateful mind is a great mind, which eventually attracts to itself great things.

> **Meister Eckhart:** if the only prayer you say in your life is 'thank you' that would suffice.

> **Deepak Chopra:** Gratitude opens the door to... the power, the wisdom, the creativity of the universe. You open the door through gratitude.

> **Marcel Proust:** Let us be grateful to people who make us happy, they are the charming gardeners who make our souls blossom.

PART II

1 – INTO THE ABYSS

When you gaze into the abyss,
the abyss also gazes into you.

Nietzsche

We have entered scary times. In the night the lump begins oozing. I try to reassure Keso when she wakes me in panic, but it is a reflex action to buy me time to emerge from my own panic, rather than a genuine engagement with what is happening. Dr Kay is off the island for Chinese New Year and so Jay phones the hospital and speaks to the urgent care duty nurse. She finds Keso's file and reads that Dr Kay has written that this might happen. I wish he'd told us! I feel myself struggling not to move to indignation and anger at Dr Kay. For a split second I find myself thinking that life would be so much easier if I could just blame someone. The nurse tells Jay that she will try and contact Dr Kay, adding that although she doesn't think that Keso is in any immediate danger, we are welcome to bring her in so that they can clean the site. Keso states emphatically that she will not be going to hospital – I can clean it!

Keso writes to her father:

So, an interesting night... Just as I was getting ready for bed, I felt a liquid on my head, which I assumed was something from the ceiling but turned out to be oozing from my lump. It was a creamy pinkish colour and smelt of rotten eggs. Had a little freak out as I didn't know what was happening but we called the hospital and they tried to get in touch with Dr Kay but he's out of the country so they spoke to the urgent care duty nurse, who said so long as I wasn't experiencing sudden pain and there wasn't a huge wound then I was welcome to come in but didn't have to. So put a towel down on my pillow and managed to get a good night's sleep. Not much leakage overnight but then in the morning we've had about an hour or so of gentle leaking. It stinks but seems to just be coming out of the pores and there's no pain. Plus the lump has gone down! The hospital says they will keep trying to reach Dr Kay but until then I don't really want to go in and have another doctor do something drastic. My scalp feels a bit weird at the moment, like saggy and dull, but my face feels less under pressure. Anyway just got to keep mopping up the fluid and hopefully the lump will disappear, and by the time I see Dr Kay I can come off the painkillers. So just going to take it easy today and let my head do what it needs to do.

And so we move ourselves from panic, anger and fear to a rational engagement with the facts. All it takes is time, awareness and surrender, to experience the return of faith.

The lump continues to discharge over the next couple of days, and we continue to do what feels right and to nurture ourselves. We do our best to keep the area clean but I will breathe a sigh of relief once Dr Kay returns. Jay prepares breakfast for Keso and organises his photographs, taken the previous day, for posting on Instagram; Keso rests, reads, does her exercises; and I go for my walk. I take the elevated walkway to the harbour and stand looking across the water to Kowloon. I am eager to explore further afield but don't want to go too far in case the situation changes. However, I also know that there is a part of me that wants to escape, to keep going until I have left this nightmare far behind me.

When I return from my walk Keso is low. She has noticed that the lump has grown again and there is now some pain, although nothing like before, but it reminds her of how far she has to go and how little is truly known about the form the journey will take or how long it will last. I know that we both have unexpressed fears. I regularly push words such as *petrified, terrified, dread, horror* out of my thoughts, clamping down on them before I become out of control with grief. I am constantly pushing images of a keening, grieving, distraught mother from my mind. It is only in the Silence that I can let these words and images be; not deny them, but move through them. Keso and I share tears, big hugs and how much we love each other. We are truly blessed to have Keso as a daughter and I need to remind her of this. Whatever the final outcome, she is loved beyond measure. I have rechristened it *the lump of love.* Despite the fact that we know so little about it, it has brought so much love into her life, and so while its here we shall love it as part of her, but we shall rejoice when it has gone! Faith, hope and love, but the greatest of these is love!

Too often we reject the conditions in our bodies that cause us pain and anxiety. I know that my body responds differently to positive affirmations than it does to negative thinking, and that it is empowering to send love to those parts that are hurting, particularly when we are doing everything else that we can. Keso is committed to taking as much control over her healing as possible; she has never been a passive patient. Love is what we need to fight the good fight.

We are still unable to reach Dr Kay and the lump continues to discharge and change shape. The smell has changed, it is sweet and sickly and is upsetting Keso's stomach, and so a very nervous mother is attempting to wash her hair again. We are all keen to have a conversation with Dr Kay. I write to Anthony:

Huge discharge in the early hours after an evening of great despair! We've saved lots in plastic bags and phoned the hospital...

I am woken around midnight by a terrified Keso standing over me eyes wide with fright and filled with tears. I try to drag myself out of my deep sleep and focus. It's that question again, 'What's happening to me, Mumma?' I look up, before I'm properly awake I hear myself respond, 'Better out than in my love!' She flops onto the bed beside me; her head and face are covered in the shiny, slimy, thick pink gunk. It is matted in her hair, her face is slick with it, and the air is pervaded with the smell of rotten eggs. Behind Keso, standing in the bedroom, Jay silently points at her pillow – it is covered in the discharge. It is impossible to describe how out of our depth we all feel. We busy ourselves doing things; anything is better than the silence and the helpless staring. We need to be pulling confidently together rather than separately falling apart.

Jay gently wipes away the liquid as it continues to ooze. I wash her face; clean her eyes, open windows to get rid of the smell. When Jay first phoned the hospital about the lump he was asked if he had kept a sample of the discharge. We hadn't and so we decide to collect some now and keep it in a box in the fridge until our appointment. I ask Jay to phone the hospital and find out if there is anything else we should be doing. The advice is the same: keep the site clean, and bring her in if anything changes.

It is early morning, we don't have much in the way of first aid in the house. I fill a bowl with warm soapy water, take the make up remover pads from the bathroom cupboard, and set about cleaning around the site. I am nervous. I don't want to hurt Keso, I don't want to cause the wound to tear, and I don't want to risk causing any further infection. I wash around and over the site as best I can, but it continues to slowly ooze. We have Betadine, an antiseptic cream that I bought from Watson's – Hong Kong's equivalent of Boots – and I apply it liberally to one of the make-up pads and place it gently on the wound. Should I leave it open to the air, or should I cover it up? Which has the least risk of infection? I don't know, but instinctively I feel we should leave it open, particularly as it continues to ooze. I hug Keso and we sit holding hands side by side on the sofa; the tears are silently running down her cheeks. I want to be positive and I want to be truthful. I bear this in mind as I gently tell her how amazing she has been, how loved and supported she is, how strong and determined she is.

I recite parts of Lynne's Treatment; remember, I say, 'God's will in you is Health and Wholeness... I know and affirm that your body is a safe place to live... you are radiant, vital and alive, all is well.' She says nothing as I continue to remind her of what she knows in her heart, but she nods and squeezes my hand. Jay comes and sits beside her and I place her hand in his; it's his turn to reassure her in his way.

I continue to support Keso in all the ways I know how. I contact Julia about holistic treatments as soon as Keso is discharged to ask for advice.

Julia writes:

> Thanks so much for the photos. They're really helpful in getting an additional sense of where Keso is, as are your detailed updates. The adjustment has to be incredibly difficult and although she's certainly proved herself to be determined, brave and resourceful, getting out of hospital and into the reality of home life, which has changed considerably, is no picnic emotionally or physically. Overwhelming doesn't cover it, I suspect. And I

completely agree with you in your position of non-intervention and waiting to see what unfolds.

There is something Keso can try of a non-intervention variety that will help to support her emotionally as she makes her way through this next stage of the healing process. You are probably familiar with Bach Flower Remedies—Rescue Remedy is the best-known one, used during an immediate trauma, but the individual essences, which are used for longer-term treatment, are equally impressive in their results. One I find extremely effective in the aftermath of trauma of any kind is Star of Bethlehem: it's the remedy of inner healing. It sustains, soothes, and centres and is indicated whenever there's been a sudden shock, accident or illness for the ensuing stress, grief, and basically when a person is completely upended. In a nutshell it helps to release the trauma and bring the person back into a state of balance.

There are some other wonderful remedies you can follow up with depending on how things go. For example, Gorse is for despondency and recovery from traumatic incident that created a state of despair and is good for psychological recovery; it is one of the most important remedies. Aspen gives trust and confidence to meet the unknown, helps with vague anxiety, apprehension, hidden fears and nightmares. Impatiens helps with the ability to flow harmoniously with time and daily rhythms, to embrace life events and the pace of others and also helps with stress and pain due to tension and resistance in the body. Oak helps to recover from severe illness, when the body and mind are exhausted, the patient is stoic but struggling with change, and despairs and chafes against the loss of control. They are strong, determined people who fight on against the odds, feel a strong sense of duty and obligation, and become frustrated if something (such as sickness) prevents them from carrying on. Gentian is the remedy for depression from known causes. Gentian and Wild Rose are something of a natural combination. They can strengthen a person's resolve and the ability to understand that all healing is a *process that it is usually cyclical in nature and never (as we always hope) linear. So the combination can help a patient withstand the ups and downs of the healing process and stay on the healing path even when faith and hope are tested.*

For now Star of Bethlehem would probably be the best to start with and is the one I'm intuitively drawn to after having sat with it for a little while. The principle is the same as homeopathy; they work on an energetic level. The good news with flower remedies is that they don't interfere with allopathic treatment, and essential oils don't interfere with how flower remedies work. Oh—and speaking of essential oils, a drop of peppermint, diluted in a drop or two of carrier oil, and rubbed over the area around her eye where there is swelling should help. But cautious application—it's miserable to get it into the eye itself. I continue to work on Keso daily, so any changes, please let me know and I'll redirect where necessary. Best of success to Keso with the marvellous Dr. Kay on Thursday, what a blessing, with tender love to you both.

We are always grateful for Julia's advice, but make our own decisions about how to proceed, 'following the guidance of the Inner Light', as Lao Tzu directs.

Four days after the lump erupts we manage to speak to Dr Kay. He is back on Hong Kong Island and has been reviewing the situation. Our relief at having him back is palpable; we are no longer treading water but are all buoyed up and ready to be part of the action once more! He phones to let us know that he has arranged for Keso to have a surgical consultation the following day with Dr Fan, a neurosurgeon with an office in the same building as Dr Kay.

Ambulances are a rare sight on Hong Kong's streets. I notice that most patients at Adventist needing support arrive and leave in personal, state-of-the-art people carriers with chauffeurs and the ever-present Filipino carer. The hospital does not appear to have a fleet of ambulances of its own and certainly we are never offered the use of one, so it's a taxi for us.

We leave for our rendezvous with Dr Fan, and Jay manoeuvres Keso into the lift in her wheelchair; their apartment is on the 10th floor. It's a tight fit with the wheelchair and us. Once down in the entrance hall we are greeted with smiles and 'dzou sen' – good morning – from the concierge. Outside Jay hails a taxi, more manoeuvring, folding and stowing of the wheelchair in the boot, and we are off to the hospital first to have the 24-hour ECG fitted.

We are met by one of the nurses who looked after Keso and she is really pleased to see how well Keso is doing. Once the telemetry is fitted, it's on to Central by taxi to see Dr Fan for a specialist opinion. Once more I am struck by the differences between public and private healthcare. We are in a very plush building with a bank of lifts. A large, marble-tiled, mirrored lift silently whisks us up from a beautifully decorated lobby to the carpeted fifth floor. We find Dr Fan's offices and are let in via entry phone by his secretary. There is a short wait before we are ushered into his large, well appointed and comfortable consulting room.

Dr Fan, a middle-aged man of average Hong Kong height, has a friendly and open face; he is wearing grey trousers and a white shirt over which he wears a charcoal grey cashmere sweater. He greets Keso first with a smile and a handshake, then Jay and me, and immediately asks our relationship to her. He is reassured that we have a right to be present at the consultation, and once Jay and I are seated he gets straight down to business.

Keso has been wearing a woolly hat whenever we go out since her discharge from hospital, partly because we are afraid of infection and partly because she wants to hide the lump. He asks permission to remove the hat. I am sitting slightly removed from Keso, Jay and Dr Fan, and so am in a good position to observe him. What I see fills me with dread. He flinches when he sees the lump, his eyes widen, his spectacles slip down his nose, his smile disappears into a frown, but then he collects himself and, expressionless, continues to feel the lump.

We begin to get more of a flavour of Dr Fan and his approach when he says very directly, 'Well Keso, this is not good, I don't know what it is but I don't like it.' Keso's eyes widen and she slumps in her chair, tears running down her cheeks. Dr Fan sits close to her and touches her arm, 'Don't worry, Keso!' he says gently. We are to hear these words from him over and over again in the next couple of months, and as now, they always reassure us. I am aware that my shoulders are almost touching my ears, and that I am holding my breath and my crossed arms tightly – I am trying to keep it together and not disappear into my fear. I have been expending so much energy on doing this that I have forgotten that Keso needs me, and Dr Fan has to ask me to come and sit with her.

The spell is broken, I am *Mumma* once more, and I have my arm around her, gently wiping her eyes and telling her she will be all right. Dr Fan gives her a moment to compose herself and then, when he's sure that he has her attention, he tells her what he intends to do. He pauses often, as she is very distressed, reassures her and waits until she can once more engage with what he is saying. He wants her to understand and be in control of her decision-making. I love this man already! He is going to readmit Keso to hospital tomorrow so that he can take a sample of the fluid in the lump, which he believes, like Dr Kay, is a sign of an infection. He is cautious about putting a needle in and wants to do it in hospital in case of bleeding from the needle, as Keso is on an anticoagulant and more susceptible to a bleed.

Before we leave he takes me aside and asks me about Anthony; 'What of the father,' he says, 'can he be here?' I tell him that Anthony has recently returned to London, but that I am sure he will want to be here given these new circumstances. He says that this would be a good idea. I am beginning to understand the seriousness of this new situation. The numbness and disconnection I experienced on that Saturday morning in February – that turned our world upside down – has returned.

Keso is tearful and very low on the journey home and throughout the evening. We are all very subdued and silent on the journey, each of us locked in our own thoughts. Jay and I do our best to support her, but we are also both affected by Dr Fan's news, and need time to process the information. There is never enough time, and it feels as if whenever I relax my guard I am suddenly called upon to respond to the next frightening event. I know that there is a difference between responding and reacting, and I also know that I don't always manage a *mindful* response. That is, one guided by reasoning, logic and faith; if I am taken by surprise then I can react defensively against the emotion of the moment. I believe I am slowly learning to maintain awareness and attention so that I can direct my conversations honestly and productively. Without denying the seriousness of the situation I try to emphasise the positives. Dr Fan is an experienced doctor, he is dealing with it rapidly, he has considered the dangers, he is being cautious and taking a sample to test, he has said it will be an overnight stay so she will be back home within twenty-four hours, and most significant, at last someone is taking notice of the lump. Keso is a young woman who likes to be in control – preferably of the situation, but if not, then of the facts. Her main concern is that no one really knows what to do about the lump or where it came from, and this is unsettling her. Keso's resilience is amazing and her condition is a great teacher to both of us, albeit a difficult one for her to engage with without some fear and rage in the moment.

On the day that Keso is readmitted to hospital, the boxes containing all Her and Jay's possessions arrive from the UK, after a journey of three months. Another reminder of the exciting things they were anticipating when they packed them a lifetime ago.

There is good news and not so good news from the hospital. The ECG discovered no irregular heartbeat. Dr Fung is very happy, and advises that Keso's cardiac rhythm is now comparable to that of a healthy person, and the wires have been removed. Dr Kay is pleased with her neurological recovery, her strength continues to improve as expected and he has no immediate concerns about her brain function. Keso is sent for another MRI and is then back in a familiar room, this time in the bed by the window. Dr Fan is about to carry out a bedside procedure to aspirate the lump on her scalp, and send the material to be analysed, which will take two to three days.

Perhaps most shocking for me is the news that Dr Fan is going to shave Keso's head before the procedure. Keso has had a thick head of long hair for most of her twenty-six years and within a few minutes it will all be gone! He cuts off her plaits, and at my request the nurse bags them and gives them to me. Keso is not at all fazed by this; she has in fact been suggesting that I cut her hair since my arrival in Hong Kong. I am the one with the problem. It is difficult to come to terms with all of these changes in my daughter; at least when I look at her she appears to be the Keso I have known and loved forever. Dr Fan shaves her head with a small, disposable battery-operated razor, which whines as he quickly and competently removes every hair. With no hair to get in the way, he gently but thoroughly washes her scalp for the first time, concentrating on the dreaded lump. He has a scouring pad much like the one that sits by my kitchen sink, and he's not afraid to use it! Once the head is clean he can proceed with the aspiration.

Truth be told, I'd rather not be here while he carries out the procedure. I'm not good at this stuff, seeing my daughter's body being invaded time and time again by painful and uncomfortable procedures. But Dr Fan says there is no need for us to leave, and I don't feel that I can go without letting Keso down – *Woman up!* I tell myself. Jay holds Keso's hand as Dr Fan injects a local anaesthetic into her head, and waits for it to take effect. Keso has always needed high doses at the dentist before she feels no pain – so Dr Fan has to administer more than he has anticipated. The needle is long and the syringe big; he removes two syringes full of pus before being satisfied. He closes the incision with a stitch and to minimise the chance of the site filling up again, bandages her head very tightly. Keso is unbelievable, so much endured already yet so stoic about it all!

The following day Dr Fan visits to inspect the abscess. More fluid has collected in the site and so he decides to re-aspirate the lump; he wants to clear up the infection. Another head-wash and Keso has to endure the procedure again. How does she do it!

I email Julia, updating her and letting her know that the Star of Bethlehem is on its way. She replies:

> *I can easily imagine Keso's reaction to being faced with a stay in hospital again, brief as it might be! I am sorry about the setback, it must feel horrendously unfair to her when she's been working so hard to make progress, but her resilience is a tremendous asset. You can use Purification to help combat any potential or existing infection, use on the bottom of the feet and on the lymph glands. One other interesting beneficial quality Purification has is dispelling negative emotions, particularly anger. Be sure to use Purification in the hospital – on hands, surfaces – for keeping all of you in pristine shape…*

> *Wonderful work on getting the Star of Bethlehem so quickly, I'm so glad that you've opted to go that direction.*

*I'm also glad that you'll have some other flower essences
in supply down the road as her needs shift. You might
want to try some Star of Bethlehem as well, given that
you have been undergoing plenty of trauma of your own.
It's easy to forget to look after the caretaker. There's a
quote of Alan Watt's that I love, 'The only way to make
sense of change is to plunge into it, move with it, and join
the dance.' My thoughts and love and encouragement are
with you as well as Keso, and light and prayers are going
out your way for outrageously good results.*

Reflections:
I sit quietly in the Silence, my refuge and my guide. Julia has put
me in touch with my own needs, which despite my experience and
wisdom, have been neglected. Trying to avoid chiding myself for
this outrageously silly behaviour, I set about identifying those
needs and finding ways to meet them. There is a tight knot high in
my stomach; I imagine it to be the size of my fist, and just as solid.
It won't move, it won't release, and it blocks the flow of food and
energy. At first I want to explain it away as a response to the new
foods and eating habits developing here in Hong Kong, and start
taking Imodium. I want it to be something with a simple and
superficial solution – after all, there's enough going on. But really I
know that it is part of my response to the traumatic situation. It sits
uncomfortably, like a fur ball, gathering more and more to itself; if
only, cat-like, I could expel it! There is a layer of anxiety that sits
above it, that never goes away, and my breathing has become
very shallow. I try to take deep, belly breaths and I try to yawn but
I can't, and this inability almost leads to panic attacks. I fall asleep
with little problem, but wake early and fully alert, ready to engage.
I review what has been happening in my body. I feel stuck, and
blocked; I am cold a lot of the time; there is a sense of stiffness
and heaviness in my body; and my breathing is for much of the
time shallow. Although I don't like to admit to it or let it linger, there
is a sense of dread that from time to time descends on me. As I sit
focusing on emptying out, I become aware that everything I am

doing to support Keso through this journey is what I myself need. I must practise what I preach! I make sure that I find time each morning to read the daily guide in my *Science of Mind* journal. At night I write my gratitude list. On my walks I often listen to satsang with Mooji, or focus on observing my thoughts come and go. I create affirmations and I adapt Lynne's treatment to reflect the truth of my circumstances. The journey of a thousand miles begins with a single step – I think I have taken quite a few...

2 – DARK NIGHT OF THE SOUL

...a deeply disturbing moment and a precious moment of transformation

Thomas Moore

I am with Keso when Dr Fan visits, familiar with his smile and sweater. We are all cautiously optimistic; the abscess is being treated and the infection is clearing up. We are therefore not prepared for what we hear next. 'It's not good, Keso,' says the forthright Dr Fan. He shows us a clipboard with scans of Keso's brain. We are told that he has discovered three abscesses on Keso's brain.

He gives us more detail about their positions, their size, the potential dangers of each, but I really can't take it in. I am looking at the horror on my daughter's face and wondering if mine is registering the same. I hope not, I want to be able to offer Keso a safe haven from this shattering news and I can only do that if I stay strong and in control of my emotions.

Dr Fan continues to talk; surgery is required, first to clean out the abscess on her scalp. He explains the procedure, but it's too much for me to take in at this time. One of the other abscesses is beneath the lump and to access it he will need to go through this area. It is crucial that he takes no 'dirty material', as he calls it, from the scalp abscess into the abscess on her brain. The initial lab tests are back and show the same bacteria in Keso's blood as previously found. Dr Fan prescribes a course of penicillin to deal with this. All three abscesses will need to be aspirated. He is an experienced neurosurgeon, the best on the island we are told later by many of his colleagues and by the nurses, but most important, we all have confidence in him. He tells us, 'one man, one disease'. In keeping with the hospital's philosophy of 'Total Health', he is treating the whole person and questions her about everything. Jay arrives and I give him the shocking news.

I don't know how, but I write the evening update:

> Dear friends, Keso's resolve and faith are being sorely tested. This evening Dr Fan showed us the results of the MRI scan. Keso has at least three abscesses on her brain. Dr Fan has been clear that surgery will be necessary. His plan at the moment is to clean out the scalp abscess, a fairly routine procedure he assures us, and make sure that there is no infected material on Keso's scalp before he goes into the other abscesses to aspirate them. He has shaved her whole head and is cleaning the area every day to be ready for surgery. He might not need to aspirate the smallest abscess as he thinks that the antibiotics might deal with it. The surgery can't happen for two days, as Keso's system needs to be free of the anticoagulants. He has said that we could expect Keso to be in hospital for about six weeks. It would appear now that perhaps the abscesses caused the stroke (CVT), rather than the other way around... Keso has had so much to deal with and this news has shaken her. However we are supporting her to express her fears and I have no doubt that her faith will return. I know you will keep the love, encouragement and support coming.

Reflections:

I sit in the Silence. For the first time I have taken fear in with me as my companion. This isn't supposed to happen, my plan is/was to leave Hong Kong in mid March, plenty of time for Keso to recover full movement, complete physiotherapy and begin thinking about her return to work. Instead I am feeling overwhelmed and defeated and very much alone; Anthony should be here, he is needed. I am exhausted, and thinking the journey is nearly over I have let my guard down, allowed myself to begin enjoying Hong Kong, watching TV with Keso and Jay, going shopping, sightseeing, doing normal things! How could I have allowed myself to be so distracted! I should have paid more attention to Keso's concerns about her unresponsive limbs. I should have insisted earlier that they investigate the lump. I should have taken Keso to hospital as soon as it erupted. I can feel myself sliding down that slippery slope towards victimhood; looking for someone to blame and settling on myself! I have become entangled in fear and negative thinking and am in danger of allowing the energy of the Victim back into my life. This practice of sitting in the Silence is my saviour. It continues to teach me how to accept what is happening rather than respond to it fearfully and give it more negative power. Acceptance doesn't mean that I have to like it; just that I don't need to expend energy – needed more positively elsewhere – denying or resisting what is happening in the moment. Sitting and breathing and allowing myself to be with the situation have calmed me. In this moment of non-resistance I feel relief and a deep sense of peace.

I am reminded of Reinhold Niebuhr's Serenity Prayer:

> God grant me the serenity to accept the things I cannot change, the courage to change the things I can, and the wisdom to know the difference.

I write:

> *Keso has her first surgery tomorrow to clean out the abscess on her scalp and stitch it up, a fairly straightforward procedure we are told. Keso is very positive and confident in Dr Fan, and this is a procedure that he has carried out many, many times. Her Hong Kong family are with her this evening as they always are, having supper together, keeping her spirits up and keeping her up-to-date with Hong Kong gossip. Her procedure is at 4 pm tomorrow HK time, 8 am GMT. If you're up and about please tune in to her frequency and send plenty of healing energy!*

Julia writes:

> *I wish the news had been better for Keso instead of a frightening infection. But she sounds in such incredibly good hands and with doctors who have a refreshing outlook on patient assessment and treatment. Young Living have a supplement they call Inner Defence which is fantastic for boosting the immune system, and I recommend it highly as a backup to the antibiotics…*
>
> *Another key thing to keep in mind for helping keep the immune system in strong fighting shape, is to keep the body alkaline. Drinking lemon juice and apple cider vinegar is recommended, and obviously avoiding acidic foods… a high-end probiotic combo would also be a good idea. I'm doing a lot of energy work on Keso, a combination of Reiki and some other techniques I've picked up along the way. Please let me know if there's anything else I can do to support you, other than continue to pray for the highest and best outcome…*

I reply:

> *As ever thank you for sharing your knowledge with us. Inner Defence is not available in Hong Kong, so I shall try and order it online. Keso is eating an 80% alkaline diet and I have just added apple cider vinegar to the list.*

There are emails and FaceTime calls and texts to and fro between Anthony and me and I know he is doing everything he can to be with us. I write to Anthony:

> *All well here, Dr Fan visited and initially expressed the idea that perhaps an operation would not be necessary. Alas on closer examination a small amount of fluid has collected and so he will. Keso says she is OK with this; she was pleased that he'd even considered the possibility of no operation. However, as 4 pm approaches she's getting more and more unsettled about small things that normally she would take in her stride. No food or drink now until after.*

After the operation I write to Anthony, Tunde and Tom, Keso's brother:

> *Op went well under local anaesthetic. All cleaned out, Dr Fan happy. She can eat and drink in about 2 hours. She has a drain in the site for a couple of days.*

I send a photo of a tired but smiling Keso head tightly bound, with the drain on her pillow filling with pink liquid. When we ask how she's doing she looks positive and smiles at us. I am overwhelmed at my daughter's fortitude – her *mental and emotional strength in facing difficulty, adversity or danger courageously.* I post a picture on Facebook of Tunde, Keso and me on an outing to Perigueux in the Dordogne during the previous summer, a reminder of happier times. It reminds me of how lucky I am and gives me something to look forward to again. Val, a good friend of ours who lives near us in both London and the Dordogne, replies: *You are such a strong person Joan the picture is lovely. There will be more photo opportunities for you all in France in the years ahead.* I hope Val is right on both counts. Each time I find myself thinking that the situation is unbearable, I observe that somehow I am bearing it.

Anthony is en route for Hong Kong. Before he takes off I send him an email:

> It's all good! I'm tired but that's to be expected under the circumstances, and it's cumulative. Dr Fan was adamant that you should go to the flat and rest a bit before coming to the hospital. I'll compromise on you having a shower and then coming. He won't be with us until 8 pm, could be later. Keso needs you to be strong and if you're tired you are more likely to be emotional, and then she'll use up precious energy worrying about you! Hope you can sleep on the plane. Looking forward to seeing you, lots of love (I would have said all but I need some for Keso). Keso has heard and endorsed the content of this email.

To her aunt Debbie and granny Doris, I write:

> Thank you so much for all the love and prayers coming our way. Keso is really being tested! She came around after the operation in a great deal of pain, but managed it herself because she wanted to save the painkiller for bedtime, so she could have a good night. She's a tough nut! Just finished feeding her small pieces of pizza for her supper, they have to be really tiny as her face is so tightly bound. Food is a good pick you up though. Anthony will be here soon!

Jess offers to meet Anthony at the airport but I am keen to do this. I want to bring him up to date before he sees Keso, and I want time alone with him. He appears quite quickly, pulling his large suitcase. We hug and kiss and I suggest that we have something to drink before we leave. We head for a juice bar I have spotted earlier and as we wait for our order to be filled he decides to get something out of his suitcase. It is then that we discover that in his hurry to get to his daughter he has picked up the wrong bag! It takes us another half an hour to retrieve the right one and to be on our way to Keso.

Yet another emotional reunion, but clearly seeing her dad has lifted her spirits, and his present brings yet another smile to her face – a red-and-white Arsenal scarf with the 'Gooners' symbol embroidered on it! Keso's spirits are further lifted by the arrival of cousin Sam, here for two weeks to take part in the Hong Kong Arts Festival in a production of *Pride and Prejudice*.

I have become a great fan of social media, Facebook in particular. It has allowed me to keep in touch with friends and family; it has provided me with the opportunity to write about what is happening, which has been very therapeutic for me; it has meant that Keso can receive support and see how much she is loved, such an important part of her healing process; it has kept me grounded providing reminders to hold things lightly: 'Do not take life too seriously, you will never get out of it alive' is one such reminder that I read! I have discovered that as with the Universe, once I am tuned in, Facebook also provides me with just what I need. This time it is an amusing piece posted by my brother-in-law Bruce called *Even God Enjoys A Good Laugh!* It is long and ends with:

> *3 proofs that Jesus was a woman:*
> *He fed a crowd at a moments notice when there was virtually no food*
> *He kept trying to get a message across to a bunch of men who just didn't get it*
> *And even when He was dead, He had to get up because there was still work to do*

It is a very funny piece, it makes me laugh; I am being supported to hold things lightly.

3 – MONEY MONEY MONEY

Money isn't the most important thing in life, but it's reasonably close to oxygen on the 'gotta have it' scale

Zig Ziglar

A post I read on Facebook seems to best sum up how I am feeling in this moment with regard to our financial situation: *All I need right now is a hug and five hundred thousand dollars in cash!*

Anthony on money:

As well as the emotional strain of the medical challenges facing Keso we are also facing major financial challenges. It became apparent very early on that Keso's work insurance policy would only cover a small part of her medical expenses. At the end of her first stay in hospital we weren't quite sure what the total bill would be, but we did know that it would have to be paid in full before Keso could leave. Luckily Joan and I had very little debt on our cards. The exit bill arrived and I headed down to the cashier rather nervously with four cards. I was able to pay the outstanding amount in full but we were now two cards down. When I landed back in London, my step-brother Giles phoned me to find out how things were. I gave him a medical update, we talked about money and I told him that with the loans we had received to date from himself,

Bruce and Camilla totalling about £5000, we would be able to manage financially. Little did I know what was about to hit us!

On her first admittance to Adventist Hospital Keso is asked for a deposit of HK$10,000 (just under £1000). As part of the admissions process she is fitted with a wrist nametag that incorporates a barcode. This barcode is scanned every time she receives a service, and a charge is then added to her account. From day one the financial clock is ticking! I soon get used to hearing the familiar 'beep' of the scanner, as Keso automatically presents her wrist.

A few days after I arrive I am presented with the first of many white envelopes containing an itemised bill for services received to the tune of HK$40,000. They respectfully request that I settle the account within three working days. I have three credit cards with me on nil balance. Anthony is always chastising me for having all my cards in my wallet, but I thank heaven for this bad habit now! I select one at random from the pack and hand it over. I have no idea what my credit limit is on any of them, but for this first payment I am pretty sure there will be no problem. I'm always grumbling about how often the limit is being raised without my requesting it, but now I am grateful for this! I am not on online banking for all of my cards, so Anthony has to search for my statements to give me my credit limits on them all. I am trying to calculate how many white envelopes I can deal with before I'm maxed out – I give up. My major focus has to be on Keso; I'm leaving calculations and contact with the insurance company to Anthony and Jay.

Each trip to the payments desk becomes like a game of poker. Which card to select? How much to go for? Trying to betray no nervousness as I suggest an amount on one card and then wait –

yes this one will accept that amount, but there's still an outstanding sum – try this one… great it's gone through!

Anthony makes his first trip to Hong Kong and the poker game continues, but we haven't needed to start on his cards yet. We are blessed with an amazing extended family and great friends and many of them contact us early on – Do we need help with plane tickets? Do you need a loan? Let us know if you need any help until you get the insurance sorted out. This sort of generosity simply overwhelms me. Anthony and I talk it through and accept the offer of loans from Bruce, Giles and Camilla, having calculated how and when we can repay it. Keso's barcode keeps 'beeping'; meals, medication, scans, blood tests, doctors' visits, physiotherapy, nursing care, boxes of tissues, surgical stockings, telemetry, intensive care, the list grows and grows… And when Keso is discharged for the first time there are out-patient charges, hire of a wheelchair and walking stick, taxis to appointments with Dr Kay and Dr Fan in their offices in Central, vitamin and mineral supplements, essential oils, homeopathic remedies…

On February 11th Anthony emails the insurance company:

I would like to check out where we are in relation to the claim. So far we have paid out approximately £9,000 and have just received another bill from Adventist for HK$92,739 (£8,250 approx.) to be paid within 3 working days.

We discover that processing the claim can only happen 'on receipt of the full set of hospital statements', i.e. on production of the final bill together with hospitalisation and surgical claim forms completed by the attending doctor. We also discover that the claims department will not deal directly with the hospital billing department; all claims have to be submitted by Keso. We are told that there is a risk with multiple claims of over- or under-charging, and that there needs to be a final total amount to present to the insurance company for review and approval by their board. They also need to make sure that there is no pre-existing or congenital condition that might have caused or contributed to Keso's hospitalisation. All of this we are told is standard practice for all insurance companies in Hong Kong.

Finally, we are informed that, as Keso was referred from Ruttonjee Hospital, we also need to submit the medical report, discharge summary and referral letter from Ruttonjee Hospital. I feel light-headed, as if I have just climbed Everest with an extremely heavy pack on my back, with the air getting thinner and thinner and with little chance of getting down soon as bad weather is approaching!

Reflections:
I sit in the Silence breathing the thin air. This is the first time I have let fear in financially and it is threatening to overwhelm me. Having grown up in a culture of free healthcare for all under the National Health Service in the UK, I feel completely at sea in the private healthcare culture of Hong Kong. My focus has been on Keso and her recovery and I have expended no energy on how this will be paid for, except to have complete faith that the money will be there when we need it. However, with the serious nature of Dr Fan's discovery and the prospect of brain surgery, I have become aware that what I thought was my faith was in part my refusal to engage with the financial reality of the situation. I have chosen to let Anthony and Jay manage this, and turned my back on it. I am reminded of Dr Fan's edict, 'one man, one disease', and my own belief in One Mind, One Life Force, One Universal Power, whether expressed scientifically or spiritually. It follows that there is therefore one situation and one solution. I cannot pick and choose which aspects to engage with, everything is interconnected and I must engage and act positively and consciously with the whole, which includes the financial circumstances, if I am to truly support Keso's recovery. I read that the more we shift our vision from fear to faith the more we are rewarded with what we desire. I believe

this, but I also know that it takes time and dedicated spiritual practice, both of which I am currently struggling with. Ernest Holmes says:

> What we should do is to consciously and persistently think that which we wish to have is ours... If we want money we must think in such a way as to bring us money. We must think we have money. We must think positively.

I can only take one step at a time so I turn my attention to positive thinking. The idea of 'I'll believe it when I see it' is replaced by 'I'll see it when I believe it'. I construct an affirmation to keep in my pocket for those moments when I am gripped by fear and negativity:

> *My faith and belief guide me; right here and now I allow and receive money and abundance from all sources known and unknown, expected and unexpected, with grace and appreciation. I trust in the Universal Law that always says YES!*

The next step is to support positive thinking with positive action.

When it is revealed that Keso will need brain surgery I write:

> *These are testing times – financially also – as the insurance company will only reimburse a certain level of expenditure. Expenditure to date has been over £32,000, and there will now be brain surgery with all its attendant costs, intensive care, medication, hospitalisation for six weeks... We are talking to the insurance company and will also get some costs from Adventist, but we may need to move her to a public hospital. Anthony is considering coming back to Hong Kong.*

Everything happens so fast. Dr Fan tells us about the abscesses and required surgery; he knows what a costly process this has been to date and he knows what is to come will be very expensive. He is able to adjust his own costs, he says, but he cannot do anything about the hospital charges, they are fixed. He tells us that he can also perform the procedure within the public hospital system. He wants to give us time to think about how we want to proceed, but we need to make a decision within the next two days – the length of time it will take for Keso's system to be free of the anticoagulants. Anthony and I are overwhelmed by how quickly the situation has escalated, and are trying to manage it while being thousands of miles apart.

While I am busy digesting information, fighting fear and holding Keso, Jess is making decisions and taking action – God bless her! She is creating an online fundraiser for Keso's treatment. It's as quick and simple as that. This is not something that I totally understand – I am out of my comfort zone with sharing financial information and asking for money publicly – but I absolutely trust Jess on this matter. We are all working in Keso's best interests, and while I don't always understand what this work consists of, I have faith that we are always being guided to the next step.

Indiegogo Fundraising for Keso

The Story
Dear Family, Friends, and Generous strangers, thanks for taking the time to visit this page. Pictured above is our beautiful, brave, and determined Keso.

In the last month she has endured a stroke, unilateral paralysis, seizures, a chest infection, a blood infection, and heart stoppages. If that wasn't enough, they've just discovered 3 brain abscesses that need surgery to be treated.

This fundraiser has been set up to raise as much money as possible to help cover Keso's medical expenses and ease the financial burden on her family.

If you would like to make a donation, that would be greatly appreciated.

If you can't donate, don't worry – prayers, positive energy, and words of encouragement are all accepted as well.

At this stage we don't know exactly how much this round of hospital care is going to cost, but anything we raise will help enormously towards the final bill. Our goal figure is based on the cost of Keso's first hospital stay.

Please feel free to share this link with anyone you think would like to donate. We've included a bit about Keso and her story so far, below. Thank you again from the bottom of our hearts.

Keso, Anthony (Keso's dad), Joan (Keso's mum), Jerome (Keso's boyfriend) and Edward & Jess (Keso's HK cheerleading squad)

About Keso
For those of you who don't know Keso personally but would like to donate, let us tell you a bit about her and why we need your help. Keso is from London and moved to Hong Kong on Dec 30th, 2014 ready to start a new year in a new place. She worked hard to reach her goal of finding a job, moving to Hong Kong, and embarking on a new adventure of a life abroad with her boyfriend. After 1 month of living in Hong Kong, Keso fell ill with what we thought was just a sinus infection. Her condition worsened and she lost movement and control of her left arm and leg. It turns out Keso had CVT – Cerebral Venous Thrombosis. In short, Keso had suffered a very rare type of stroke.

Her parents flew from London to Hong Kong to be by her side and what followed was a roller coaster ride of chest infection, blood infection, seizures, heart stoppages, and a stay in Intensive Care where we celebrated her 26th birthday. Keso has bravely battled through each of these obstacles and has begun to regain movement in her arm and leg. She was finally discharged and allowed home. Her hospital bill was around £32,000 (approx. $400,000+ HKD). We thought the road to recovery had begun with Keso just needing to concentrate on getting her strength *back and doing physio. After only 10 days out of hospital, Keso has now had to return after they discovered she has 3 abscesses on her brain. These infections have to be dealt with and surgery is needed. This involves another 6 weeks in hospital, MRIs, doctors' fees, scans, medications, ICU, and more. Another sizeable hospital bill is on the horizon and that is why we're hoping to raise enough money to cover as much of these upcoming costs. We don't want Keso to worry about money; we just want her to concentrate on getting well so that she can return to the adventure she moved here for. In the face of all of this she has remained positive, and her determination and attitude have been an absolute inspiration to us all.*

Over the phone Anthony and I discuss whether or not Keso will be able to stay in Adventist, Anthony promises to get back to me within twenty-four hours. While I wait he contacts Giles who says that we mustn't move Keso, he and Lisanne will deal with any shortfall in the finances. When Anthony phones me at midnight to give me this good news I burst into tears. Once again I am overwhelmed at such kindness.

I write to Giles and Lisanne:

You know exactly how much your generosity means to us because you also have children for whom you never believed that your greatest wish would simply be life. My love and gratitude for such an amazing act of love.

Knowing that the next bill could easily reach five figures, once more Giles comes to our rescue; within twenty-four hours he has transferred a significant sum to our account.

Anthony meets Jay's parents at the airport before his flight back to Hong Kong. They shower him with love and money for Keso collected from the Canlas extended family and friends. Anthony emails Jay: You have amazing parents; I had such a supportive caring talk with them before boarding. I am weighed down with the love they are sending…

I distance myself physically from the fundraiser – I'm afraid that I might get caught up in checking up on who is giving and how much. I have a strong Critic and Judge in me, and although I am now more aware of them, in moments of stress and fear they can take over, and I would hate to find myself, and my relationships with friends and family, at their mercy. Everyone following Keso's journey has given so much already. But I am keeping an eye on how much is being raised.

My friend Carol posts:

> My friend Joan Kendall's lovely daughter Keso is currently in hospital in Hong Kong awaiting brain surgery after suffering a rare thrombosis which has resulted in 3 blood clots needing to be aspirated. The family's insurance has covered her hospitalisation for the past 5 weeks or so, but the surgery is not covered and is very costly. I am sharing this Indiegogo campaign, which has been initiated to help them out with financing her treatment. Some of you will know Joan as the weaving member of Women of the Cloth and may feel you want to help out too, even with a tiny amount as it all adds up. It could be any of us parents finding ourselves in this position. Sending love and best wishes to Joan, Keso and the whole family at such a stressful time.

Individuals in South London Women Artists also respond generously sending love, good wishes and money.

I email Candice, one of Keso's friends from school, asking her to post something about Keso's situation on the Haberdasher Askes Hatcham school site (their secondary school) and we receive more donations. Asking for money is a new experience for me and takes me way outside of my comfort zone, and to deal with my discomfort I write:

We know that not everyone is in a position to contribute money and we are always open to 'currency' in the form of love, healing energy, positive thoughts, and other forms of practical help...

Jess posts several updates, one of which identifies what the money is being used for:

Once again THANK YOU for the support and donations. Your kindness is overwhelming and humbling. In case you are wondering what your money will be going towards, here are some examples of Keso's expenditure to date:
- *MRI $14,390 HKD (approx $1800 USD) [x 1]*
- *CT Scan $4630 HKD (approx $590 USD) [x 2 so far]*
- *Special Care Room Post Operation $7,000 HKD (approx $900 USD) [1 night]*
- *Bed on Surgical Ward $800 HKD (approx $100 USD) [per night – 12 so far]*
- *Pharmacy [medication so far] $17,000+ HKD (approx $2000 USD)*
- *Operation room (first procedure) $10,179 HKD (approx $1311 USD)*
- *Operation room (second procedure) $35,173 HKD (approx $4500 USD)*

The actual surgery fees and doctors' fees, which we have yet to be billed for, will be the biggest expenses. We have 6 days left of our fundraiser so there is still time to share the link – whether we meet our goal or not, we are truly grateful for every dollar that has been raised.

Anthony does some soul-searching and makes the difficult decision to send an email to some business acquaintances with whom he has worked for a long time. It is not an easy step for him to take, as it challenges his own ethics and value base. Also he is used to helping and supporting others – he is Chair of several charities and has been involved in community development for decades – being on the receiving end is a very new experience for him!

He writes:

May I start by saying that I thought long and hard before writing this email, but realized that I had to put my concerns/pride to one side for a greater consideration. Some of you may know that our daughter Keso has been gravely ill in hospital in Hong Kong. She set off on her great adventure to live and work in Hong Kong at the end of last year full of excitement and anticipation of the life she and Jay (her boyfriend) would have here. By the end of January she was admitted to hospital having lost movement on the left side of her body and with severe head pains, only to be diagnosed with a rare form of stroke – Cerebral Venous Thrombosis – which has a one in 2 million chance of occurring. Following the diagnosis she has endured, the stroke and unilateral paralysis, but also seizures, pneumonia, a blood infection and heart stoppages. If that wasn't enough, they more recently discovered 3 abscesses on her brain that require complex surgery.

Keso was 3 weeks into her new job when this happened, and although she has health insurance via her employers this is not at the level that will take care of such a 2 million to 1 tragedy. We have so far paid out over £32,000 on medical bills alone, with no guarantee of reimbursement. Keso had been discharged from hospital when the 3 brain abscesses were discovered and this meant immediate re-admittance and brain surgery with all its attendant high costs. This second period of hospitalization is likely to cost between £30,000 and £40,000 and we are very uncertain as to whether or not this will be fully covered by Keso's insurance policy. Keso's close friends have set up a Crowdfunding page to help us meet the costs and we have been overwhelmed by the response from friends, family and some complete strangers. To date this has raised $20,000 US, but this still falls far short of the amount we estimate will be *needed to meet the final bill. As I am not involved in the management of the fundraising it might be that you have already donated, in which case my grateful thanks go to you. If you are in a position to make a donation of whatever size we would be most grateful.*

The fundraiser runs for fifteen days and raises $35,026 US (£25,000 approx). Jess has set a target of $50,000 US and we are delighted at the response. We also receive cheques and bank transfers from people who don't trust the Internet – several people wisely check with us to make sure it isn't a scam before donating. On top of this we are blown away by the donation of an amazing five-figure sum from a generous friend!

As I write this I pick up a copy of *The Science of Mind Guide to Spiritual Living*; it falls open at a page bearing the heading 'Surrender to the Inflow of Prosperity'. I read:

Surrendering to the Divine inflow of abundance is the first step in growing our prosperity... Surrendering... is not giving up or giving in. Rather, it is stepping aside and allowing the Divine so fully into our consciousness that our life is taken over by Its Presence. Then the unlimited abundance of Spirit demonstrates as our ever-increasing prosperity.

I like these words; in the face of adversity we did not give up and we did not give in, we did what we could to the best of our ability, and then stepped aside and waited...

4 – IN THE HERE AND NOW

Held firmly in the grip of here and now I am lived a moment at a time
A life time's learning contained within the routine of each 24-hour cycle
I unfold and extend with each new breath as I find I am in service to Life
Life in the form of the beautiful old woman who sits and knits
Waiting for her daughter to return from surgery
With whom I share smiles my weaving and she in turn her knitting
And in lieu of language a universal thumbs up
Life in the form of the nurses with us throughout this white-knuckle ride
A constant reminder of our purpose – to care and to serve
Life in the form of the doctors through whose fingers healing flows
And Life in the form of my daughter whose courage has been astounding
Whose faith though often challenged by fear and uncertainty
Continues to light her way through each day
– And at the heart of all –
The ebb and flow of love connecting and sustaining us
In the here and now...

Anthony is back with us just in time to give Keso a boost before the big day. We receive so many amazing emails, posts and texts bringing us courage, strength, healing, love and peace:

> **Karen:** *I am heading to bed now sending love and prayers to you and your beautiful, courageous daughter Keso. Sending strength and focus to her wonderful surgeon and team. Know that you are held...*

Sandra & Wally: *Our prayer wheels are spinning for Keso – and it's important that the lemon tree has burst into blossom. We send courage and strength and healing…*

Barbara & Mark: *Just behind you, not yet detectable by human camera technology, stands an army of healing angels to carry you along. And out here the rest of us bearing love too…*

Vanessa: *Please know that the ripples reach far and wide and we are a tower of strength behind you and your loved ones: we are there behind and around you…*

Andy: *We are praying hard at this end for complete healing…*

Clothilde: *Step by step. Lève le poing et dit 'j'y arriverai!'*

Keso has asked for the details of the procedure; she finds having detailed information reassuring. Dr Fan explains the whole procedure to her and adds that if the abscesses refill he may have to repeat the procedure, something that none of us want to contemplate! She holds my hand and confides that she is terrified; tears pour down her cheeks. 'I don't want to die, Mumma!' she cries. What do I say to her? I am being sorely tested; do I really believe the teachings that I have been pursuing and absorbing for decades? This is a moment when only the Truth will do. I tell her simply that I do not want her to die either but that Life as we both know is Eternal and Infinite, continuing beyond the existence of the body. I remind her of the beautiful Treatment that Lynne sent her:

> *God's will in you is health and happiness… you are radiant, vibrant and alive… Keso, don't forget these words, there is so much love surrounding you, you will come through this Keso!*

Keso is moved to the Special Care ward, ready to undergo a stereotactic biopsy to aspirate two of the three abscesses. This is a procedure using a computer and imaging to find and concentrate on a particular site, and in this case, guide the removal of material using a fine needle to aspirate the site. Dr Fan and his colleague Dr Yu have done the complex math to calculate the angle of trajectory. The procedure starts at 8 am, the first stage being to screw a metal frame into her head at four points to help position the stereotactic device and hold it in place. For this Keso is given a local anaesthetic, but during the procedure – which is carried out with her in an upright position – she faints. Dr Fan is slightly alarmed by this, but on questioning her to find out if this has happened to her in any procedures before, he is relieved when she tells him that she has sometimes passed out when giving blood.

Once everything is in place a CT scan reveals that the two larger abscesses have decreased in size, as a result of the antibiotics, but disappointingly the smallest abscess has increased. As the scalp abscess appears clean and is healing well, Dr Fan changes his plan and decides to drain all three abscesses. This part of the operation lasts four hours. They will use a light anaesthetic so that they can bring her round quickly after the surgery and make sure that no mistakes were made, and that all parts of the brain are still functioning well.

Anthony and I decide to go for a walk along the Bowen Trail. We need the fresh air and change of scenery, and sitting around waiting will do nothing to lower our level of anxiety. We walk all the way to the pagoda at the Wan Chai Gap, and then sit and watch people in their daily Tai Chi practice. Some have music to accompany their slow, gentle, fluid movements and it is comforting to listen and to watch. We hold hands and talk…

We return to the hospital anxious but full of hope. It has been a taxing four hours for us, but how has our daughter fared? We sit in the visitors' room anxiously waiting. Jay paces up and down outside, alert to every arrival of the lift. Suddenly he shouts, 'It's Keso, she's here!' We rush to see her as they wheel her out of the lift. Keso has returned to the ward in some pain and discomfort and covered in wires, drain, drip and catheter, head tightly bound, but smiling as always despite the gruelling procedure. We are so happy to see her.

Within hours of the procedure she is sitting up, eating, talking and moving her left arm and leg. The surgery has been a success! The abscesses have been drained and Dr Fan is pleased with how the procedure went. He tells us that it is now all about rest and gentle exercise, and he orders another CT scan for tomorrow to make sure that the abscesses are not refilling. If all is well she will be moved back to the surgical ward. It is after the surgery and with the knowledge that it might have to be repeated that Anthony makes the decision to write the email to his business acquaintances and friends.

The CT scan shows that there has been no damage to Keso's brain, and that the abscesses are not refilling. We are beyond grateful! Dr Fan tells Keso to move about as much as she can and to start physiotherapy immediately so that he can monitor her neurological functioning. The white stockings make their reappearance, but this time on both legs. Dr Fan removes one layer of Keso's dressing, which provides a massive relief of pressure on her head. She is now on a twice-daily dose of Rocephin (antibiotic), Ultra-Ce for the pain, and Keppra, (anti-epileptic), which has been upped to a double dose. As her condition improves she is returned to the surgical ward.

I write:

A bad night, very uncomfortable with the very tight head bandages, the ECG wires for monitoring her heart, blood pressure monitor and the catheter! Cheered up after a good breakfast and after all were removed. The physiotherapist has visited and taken her through her paces. It's 7.30 pm and Keso is waiting for her supper sitting up chatting with Jay. Another layer of tight bandaging has been removed, let's hope she has a good night's sleep tonight!

With finances on our mind Anthony sends the following email to the insurance company:

I wish to enquire about the claim that has been submitted to you. You should have the full costs and information concerning Keso Kendall's first hospitalization. Is there any further information you require from us or from the hospital? If there is this needs to be dealt with urgently as the principle doctor for this claim is going away for a month. Unfortunately Keso has been readmitted to hospital for a major surgical procedure. Could you please advise us what level of cover the policy offers for this?

We get a response the following day:

This is a substantial claim amount; we are talking about $310,000 HK (approx. £26,500). As this is a new policy we need to undertake a thorough assessment. We are dealing with it as a priority.

They inform us that they need to contact other insurers covering Hong Kong to make sure that Keso has not made other claims – in other words, that this isn't a fraudulent claim. They send us their benefits schedule outlining various entitlement levels for a range of services, including accommodation, doctors' fees, operating theatre charges, room and board, physicians' hospital visits, specialists' fees and miscellaneous charges. Jay studies these carefully to make sure that we are claiming under the right headings and to see if we can perhaps claim under headings that have not as yet reached their maximum. It is a painstaking task, and Jay is absolutely the right man for the job.

Keso has a haemorrhoid, her first ever, and Dr Fan prescribes laxatives and medication to treat it. The nurse arrives to apply the medication and discreetly pulls the curtains around the bed as we wait nearby. My daughter lets out a blood-curdling scream that brings me running, and I hastily inform the nurse that the laxative will be sufficient. Poor Keso, to have come through so much to be nearly defeated by a haemorrhoid! She decides to apply the medication herself.

Keso's physiotherapy steps up apace and includes lunges, squats and tucks. She also does five laps of the surgical floor with her walking aid. Dr Fan wants her to start using her mental faculties. 'This is the best way to know if you are making a full recovery, Keso', he says, and so she is undertaking secretarial duties for her father, writing emails, etc. He also wants her to up her intake of calories, an instruction Keso is only too happy to comply with; she promptly orders a burger and fries for her supper. Friends come to visit and it is so good to see her chatting and joking and being enthusiastic. Sessions in the gym are proving productive and Keso is able to stand and take a few steps without the use of her walking aid!

Dr Kay visits. We have not seen him for a while as Dr Fan has now taken the lead in Keso's care. Dr Kay has always been friendly and informal with us, but on this visit he appears more subdued than usual and after carrying out a few tests of his own on Keso, with little engagement with us, he asks us to sit down. He appears uncomfortable but determined and tells us that even though Keso was making such a good recovery from the paralysis, with hindsight perhaps it was not such a good idea to discharge Keso at Chinese New Year without requesting a scan to check on the lump, and he apologises. We are all speechless for some moments – we have never received an apology from a doctor before, and are not quite sure how to respond. Anthony recovers first and thanks Dr Kay and assures him that our focus is on Keso's continued recovery, in which he – Dr Kay – has been instrumental.

As well as recognising him as a skilled and experienced practitioner, we are all very fond of Dr Kay and the particular interest he has taken in Keso's case. We have nothing but respect and admiration for him. He assures us that he will continue to monitor her condition while Dr Fan is away; his prognosis and expectations remain that Keso will make a full recovery, perhaps only struggling with regaining full use of the intricate movements of her left hand. He also tells us that he will not be charging a fee for his services from now on.

Over the next few days Keso continues to make good progress with her physiotherapy. She gains more control over her ankle and her walking improves. She has graduated to a walking stick and now eats lunch in the canteen some days, which requires a walk up and down six flights of stairs! It would have been eight, but the fourth floor does not exist, as the sound for four in Chinese is similar to the sound for death, and so is considered to be unlucky – hence no fourth floor.

She continues to eat herself well around the world, with her favourite foods coming from Calimex (Mexican), Butcher's Club (burgers) and Kelly's Cake Bop (Korean). Her biggest battle is trying to get the doctors to agree to her going home. She is on a five-week course of antibiotics twice daily and cannot face the prospect of spending this amount of time in hospital. Keso has a semi-permanent IV cannula inserted into a vein in her arm through which the antibiotics are administered twice daily. It is a nuisance showering, changing, just moving about, and it soon understandably becomes a focus for her negativity.

The daily showers continue. I am tired and working in the cramped space that is the shared bathroom provides me with challenges and a daily workout, but we both look forward to this time together. It provides me with the opportunity to get up close and personal with my daughter, and gauge how she is doing emotionally. The main focus in the hospital is on her physical recovery, but mine is on her emotional and spiritual well-being. The time we spend alone is good time for a pep talk or for exploring what else is going on in her. I don't think I have answers for Keso to the inevitable but as yet unspoken *Why?* question. She has to find these for herself, but I can remind her where to look, I can listen as she finds her own mode of expression, I can sit with her in the Silence. I don't want to take the spiritual and emotional pain away, I want her to go through it and emerge the other side stronger and with more awareness of who and what she truly is.

I write:

> *Dear friends, another request; Keso has to have large doses of antibiotics twice a day. Her veins get sore and eventually refuse to take the antibiotic, and so the nurses have to change site often. This is a painful process, and sometimes a bit hit and miss. Would you join me in 'asking' her amazing veins to allow the life saving liquid to flow easily without let or hindrance, and should a change of vein be necessary, that the process be swift and painless…*

Cousin Angela replies suggesting that we might consider a PICC line – a peripherally inserted central catheter, of which she has positive feedback. I read that this is a hollow tube; it is inserted into one of the large veins of the arm near the bend of the elbow. It is then threaded up into the vein until the tip sits in a large vein just above the heart and the medication is fed through this into your system. Like the cannula, it is flushed regularly to prevent it becoming blocked and the cap at the end of the line is changed weekly to reduce the risk of infection. Keso nearly faints when I read her this description! So we stay with the cannula – but thank you, Angela, for the suggestion.

There are regular blood tests; results show that everything that needs to is going down, confirming all is well. Dr Fan examines the site and there are no leakages; he is happy and so are we. He is going to Japan, and during his absence Dr Kay and Dr Yu will monitor Keso's progress. She is feeling much more positive, enjoying the challenge of her physiotherapy and developing a healthy appetite. On the strength of this Anthony and I decide that we are due some rest and relaxation, and so we take the afternoon off and catch a ferry to Kowloon. Kowloon is on the mainland across Victoria Harbour. Once a separate city, it was acquired by the British in 1860 and returned to China with the rest of the colony in 1997. It is now a shopping, arts and entertainment district.

Even though the harbour is now crossed by railway and road tunnels, we prefer to take the slower, scenic route offered by the Star Ferry. These old English-built double-decker steamboats, operating for over 100 years, are a throwback to a bygone era. They run frequently, ticket prices are approximately $2.00HK (approx. 18p), and it takes about ten minutes to travel across the harbour. We walk the busy streets, accosted regularly by men trying politely to sell us fake designer handbags, and then stroll along the waterfront in the sunshine, pretending to be tourists! It has the atmosphere of our own South Bank back home in London, with stalls, performers and photographers all making a bid to sell their wares.

I write:

> A good night's sleep, despite having another short-stay roommate. The nurse had to change the intravenous feed to Keso's right hand, which she was not happy about, but the new vein seems to have taken to the feed very well. There were a few anxious moments – but thankfully a painless switch. Another good physiotherapy session with

lots of stepping squats and tiptoes. Yuka, her physiotherapist, has given Keso a cane to walk with and is rigorous about making her take even strides with both legs. She doesn't want her to get into bad habits and an uneven gait. Keso has improved control over her toes and foot and hopefully the ankle will follow. Dr Yu took off the very tight bandages this morning and the wound is healing nicely, he's changed her headgear and now she looks like kitchen staff in her white, netted hat. We lunched in the cafeteria again and Dr Kay comes to join us. They are considering home leave/day release for Keso, but Cinderella-like she has to be back in time for her antibiotics. No decision will be made until Dr Fan's return though. Things must be improving; I've brought my weaving in to keep from feeling bored.

I have asked Jay to buy me a medium-sized picture frame on his next trip to IKEA; this will make a good frame for weaving on. Next I set about finding some warp (the vertical threads on a loom) and weft (the yarn woven horizontally over and under the warp). There is a local wool shop with a large but disappointing range of natural woollen yarns, that does however stock some interesting variegated cotton yarns in a range of vibrant colours. I buy these for the weft and a plain colour for the warp – not ideal, as a warp yarn really needs a high twist to it, and cotton has no elasticity and is therefore difficult to put under tension. I buy a couple of bodkins to use to weave with, as I have no bobbins, the traditional means of carrying the weft across the loom. Now that Keso is more mobile and independent I feel it is time to give her some space and weaving allows me to do this. It also provides another much-needed focus for me, which helps to address my stress levels. I have warped up a smaller frame for Keso and have bought some thicker yarns that are easier to work with so that she can weave. This is great physiotherapy for the fingers and will help her get her dexterity back. As I weave my first Hong Kong piece I imagine those synapses in the brain firing away trying to deliver messages to Keso's limbs! And this is reflected in the finished piece. Keso also gets into the rhythm of weaving and develops total control over her loom. Much as I enjoyed being able to weave again, and the interest of doctors and nurses, it is disappointing not having the proper equipment.

My very good friend Camilla offers to send me some wool from the UK. She knows how important the physical act of weaving is for me. As well as being relaxing and totally absorbing, it's a meditation that has the power to transform and transcend. I have discovered a local arts and crafts shop here, a small Aladdin's cave stuffed full of a range of creative materials, and tucked out of the way in the corner on the floor, I stumble upon a small stack of wooden looms a few inches larger than an A4 picture frame, grooved top and bottom ready to take the warp. Amazingly they cost about £3 each! One is all I need. It is a good size, and I can use it on my lap leaning it against the table in Keso's apartment; it is also very portable if I want to use it in the hospital. This loom is the only weaving equipment that this shop stocks, and so everything else is improvised. Searching online I discover a small company in Australia that makes weighted bobbins and sells them for about half of the price I would pay in the UK. I order four; I am determined to give them a try. The wool arrives with Anthony on his return to Hong Kong, beautiful autumnal shades of 100% wool in a range of ply (thicknesses). I have some ideas for the next piece, but shall wait until the right one presents itself.

It is Jay's birthday! This is the third birthday celebration since Keso was first admitted to hospital, and we are getting used to celebrating in unusual ways. For Jay, Keso and I organise a picnic in the middle of the car park under a covered seating area – it is the hospital's only outside space. Later on we have tea in the canteen to accompany a selection of Jay's favourite cupcakes, bought on my way to the hospital. Anthony and I bought Jay's present on our afternoon off in Kowloon. We spent an enjoyable half an hour in Swindon Books before deciding on a novel set in

Wan Chai and a three-dimensional paper model of the Hong Kong waterfront. Unfortunately half of Team Keso has left for Shanghai – Edward has photos in a Nike exhibition there, and so Jay's birthday celebration is a low-key affair. Anthony and I are off to see cousin Sam in *Pride and Prejudice* this evening. I think Keso and Jay are looking forward to a romantic evening *à deux* – something of a rarity these days.

I write:

> *Three steps forward, one step back today. Keso has been experiencing some pain over the past twelve hours, mainly around the sites of the pins that held the frame for her operation and in the area of the scalp abscess. The nurses ask Keso to identify her pain on a scale of one to ten. I don't know how helpful this is, but I have begun doing the same. Despite her struggle with pain over the past couple of months Keso has never gone higher than a four, no doubt determined not to let it overwhelm or defeat her.*

> *She tells Dr Yu about the pain on his morning visit and he decides to send her for an MRI scan rather than wait until the end of the week, which had been the original plan. This decision, though a wise one, frightens Keso, who starts to imagine the worst, and for a while loses her resolve and positivity. She has come through so much and just can't bear the thought of losing sight of the finish line. When Dr Kay arrives post scan, she is still very low and is further dispirited by the news that while the antibiotics appear to be working – as the abscesses are much smaller – it looks as if they are trying to refill. Nevertheless Dr Kay is adamant that all signs continue to point in the right direction. However, the possibility of further surgery will be left to Dr Fan to decide upon his return. One piece of good news – the insurers have been in touch and a payment is expected tomorrow!*

Despite the ups and downs of the day, Keso is refreshed by a good night's sleep. Dr Yu visits and changes her dressings. He reassures Keso that all signs from the scan appear positive, the new collection of liquid he suspects is sterile. In his opinion – although Dr Fan will have to confirm it – no further surgery will be required. With this good news Keso goes happily to her physiotherapy session – without the use of her stick. However, Jay keeps it nearby, just in case. Back on the ward it's on with writing practice and weaving. What a difference a day makes!

Julia writes:

> *Fantastic news all round! Cake for everyone! That is progress of the best sort. And it's lovely to see the weaving in progress – multi-level good therapy. Keep up the brilliant work, all of you!*

Anthony and I are on our way to the theatre which, as with most things, is in walking distance of the apartment. We are looking forward to the play and to supper with Sam afterwards. We discover that this is the night for the school parties! We are surrounded by the equivalent of sixth formers; no doubt this play is part of their English curriculum. The theatre is well appointed with good acoustics and comfortable chairs, and the young people are well behaved. The themes of class, money and marriage are obviously familiar ones for our young audience, and produce much laughter – particularly when Mrs Bennett exclaims, to much applause, 'Imagine, Mr Bennett, £3000 a year!' It's a very enjoyable performance and a bit of normality in our lives, and we tuck into a tasty meal afterwards with Sam.

Everything continues to flow smoothly; Keso continues to improve her walking up and down stairs and along a straight line. The physiotherapist is delighted with her progress, and the IV site has been changed with no problems. We're threatening to leave, as we're almost redundant.

In this world nothing lasts forever, and the scales have tipped again. Keso now has two roommates, one of whom is a very elderly lady who appears quite ill. It looks as if her care will be demanding on the nurses, who are already in and out frequently, attending to her needs. At first Keso is able to laugh light-heartedly with the nurses about the situation as they come and go, but as the evening progresses she feels more and more anxious about getting a good night's sleep. Keso is very agitated and close to tears; we cannot leave her like this. We ask the nurses if it is possible for her to sleep in another room, but this does not appear to be an option. We wander up and down the corridor looking into empty rooms, but then realise that they are empty because there is a massive room-cleaning programme underway. Anthony and I stay for as long as we can and then leave Jay to settle Keso for what looks like a stormy night.

I arrive to a very unhappy Keso in the morning. Tears flow almost non-stop for a very long time. The elderly lady has been screaming and shouting all night long, nurses in and out, lights going on and off, and when Keso needs to use the bathroom it is occupied by the lady's granddaughter who is having a shower! Poor Keso is distraught from lack of sleep when I get there. Wisely Dr Yu has granted her home leave – I suspect one look at her face helped him to make the right decision. I text Anthony, who is back at the apartment: *They've given her home leave, can you check that it's covered in her policy please.* I've finally got to grips with the private healthcare system and am being much more proactive!

For the home leave we decide to take Keso and all of her belongings. After a fortnight her corner of the room has become crammed with a variety of items: books, looms, yarn, toiletries, boxes of tissues, clothes, laptop, iPad, various chargers, walking stick, things to snack on... the list is endless and the fridge is overflowing with goodies. We decide to pack it all up and take it home; if she is to come back (and good luck with that, Dr Fan), then we can begin again.

The nurses are surprised to see all the bags and remind us that Keso is only allowed out for the day. 'Yes,' we say, 'it's OK, we'll be back this evening.' They look relieved. I guess none of them were looking forward to telling Dr Fan that Keso had absconded! We load all her belongings into a taxi and set off for Wan Chai and home. 'What a mess,' she comments on entering her apartment – so reassuring! She has already returned to the Keso we know and love! Keso revels in being back home, she plumps cushions, organises her cuddly animals, sets up her laptop and sighs with delight; but I feel a massive spring clean is not far off. Anthony takes her back to the hospital for her evening dose of antibiotics and she is allowed home again to sleep. Dr Fan is due back tomorrow and longer-term decisions will be made then.

Jess and Edward return from Shanghai bearing gifts, and we have a long day at the hospital to look forward to.

We arrive at 9 am for the antibiotics and expect a meeting with Dr Fan at midday. However, Dr Fan becomes delayed in an emergency operation, we are told he will be with us at 3 pm and then we are told he will be out of theatre at 6 pm, and that he wants us to wait and see him then. As you can imagine, nine hours of waiting does not make for a happy or calm Keso! We think she's entitled to a little strop every now and then, so we indulge her, and the three of us set off to the canteen for ice creams. All that is needed to bring her back into full good humour is watching Arsenal beat West Ham on *Match of the Day* on the laptop. Sometimes I seriously wonder if she is my daughter!

Dr Fan has arrived finally at 8 pm, so happy to see Keso walking. He removes the dressing to examine her head. On feeling her scalp he can see that some liquid has accumulated again so decides to aspirate, and so it is once more needle in liquid out on the spot. How does she stay so calm and accepting? I can't bear to see yet another procedure on my daughter's head and so I slip quietly out of the room. Wonderfully cousin Sam arrives for a visit, and I am delighted to have company and distraction as I wait.

Keso once more looks like the mummy from the Indiana Jones movie. She and Dr Fan are going head to head on the subject of her discharge – we always knew this would be a battle. Dr Fan's argument is that the antibiotics need to be administered on the ward by nurses who have been trained in the procedure, rather than in outpatients with whoever happens to be on duty. In football terms, this is a score draw. However, Dr Fan discovers that it is possible to administer the antibiotics safely in outpatients. We're all exhausted but what a result! Keso can leave the hospital; she's going home and she's happy. Outpatients from now on – thank you, Dr Fan! It's time to settle Keso's account, but we have been told that Adventist doesn't accept personal cheques and so there's a brief stop at HSBC on the way home to make a hefty cash withdrawal – ouch!

Somewhere between the aspiration of the scalp abscess and the procedure on Keso's brain, Instagram posts the image of Keso taken by Jay and used on the fundraiser. It is chosen by Instagram's Community Team as part of the 'Weekend Hashtag Project – Everyday Heroes'. Everyone with an Instagram account sees this. It gets over 480,000 likes. There are amazing supportive comments – 6,306 of them to be exact; and more donations to the fund. Later, when Keso is out of hospital, there is a feature printed in *Time Out Hong Kong*, which names Keso and Edward as two of the top ten Instagrammers in Hong Kong. It seems that Keso has made good use of her short time here.

Jay posts:

> *Thank you, Merci, Grazie, Danke, Arigato, Takk,*
> *Obrigado, Asante Sana, Salamat. There are many ways*
> *of expressing gratitude – I hope that in time I'll learn*
> *enough to express my thanks to all of you for the*
> *generosity, love and support you have shown. Keso has*
> *been discharged from hospital, we seem to be through*
> *the worst, and the road to recovery can now start in*
> *earnest.*

Reflections:

I sit and let the Silence embrace me once again. There is nothing more I can do and so I feel myself gently sliding into the deep, dark healing waters of surrender. Only here do I find relief. I have met death before while caring for my father in his last days, and unexpectedly been renewed by the painful encounter.

> *...Caring for him finally*
> *There were no dark hidden places*
> *As bit-by-bit the Light illumined everything*
> *And being fully who he was*
> *I embraced him and loved him fully...*

But my father was eighty-nine, accepted a diagnosis of stomach cancer, and had lived a long life in which he made a difference on both the private and public stage, as a local councillor and twice Mayor of Lewisham, finally receiving the award of Freedom of the Borough. My daughter is twenty-six and just beginning to find her way. In the days, weeks and months I cared for my father I wrote about death a lot. I needed to allow my fears a voice so that they would not consume me, so that I could avoid the familiar stress response of fight, flight or freeze. Through the writing I came to better understand death and – I thought – befriend her. But here I am, my faith once more being tested, only able to see death from one side, that of loss.

Ernest Holmes teaches that there is One Universal Life Force, expressing Itself through all beings. He goes on to say, 'the same Consciousness that expressed Itself through loved ones who have moved on, is now expressing Itself through every being around me.' I remember reading this in my studies and nodding my agreement. However, in this moment what I want most is my daughter to live and the One Life Force to express in Its unique way through Keso in the here and now – no one else will do!

Ernest Holmes also wrote that 'Life is a mirror and will reflect back to the thinker what she thinks into it.' And so firmly believing this, I recite Lynne's spiritual mind Treatment, feeling the truth of it in each word.

5 – WAN CHAI AND THE ROAD TO RECOVERY

*Always remember that your present situation is not your final
destination, the best is yet to come...*

Unknown

It's March 16th and we are settling into being back home in Wan
Chai. Keso and Jay are sleeping on the sofa-bed, so that they can
have the TV and friends around without disturbing us, and we are
in their very comfortable bed. Emails continue to arrive from
friends and family who have just heard about what has happened
to Keso, and I reply to all of them:

> *Thank you for your email; it has been a shocking time for
> all of us. I have been here since February 1st and
> Anthony is on his second 'tour of duty' following the
> devastating discovery of abscesses on her brain. At this
> moment everyone is happy with her recovery. She is now
> able to walk short distances without her stick and has
> regained a lot of control over her left (dominant) hand,
> although her writing skills need more attention. Her
> emotions as you can imagine fluctuate a lot, and
> unexpected delays or setbacks can send her into tears
> and rage, but this is only to be expected. We have had
> overwhelming support and loving wishes from friends,
> family and even strangers from around the world. This*

has been immensely important to us – Team Keso – and to Keso's recovery. You are now copied into our daily updates.

The only thing I haven't come to terms with is the level of light pollution and nightlong activity in the centre of Hong Kong – it truly is a city that never sleeps. I have taken to wearing a blindfold/ sleep mask at night, and it does the trick.

It has been decided that Keso's treatments will be at 9 am and 9 pm, and Jay goes with Keso for her first morning appointment in the outpatients department. They arrive and check in at the appointment desk, and take a seat until she is called. From there they are shown into the treatment room by the nurse, the line is flushed with a saline solution, the pouch of Rocephin is connected, and the tap turned on; all that's left is to sit and watch as the antibiotic slowly drips through the line into Keso's bloodstream. Another flush, the cap replaced, the site protected from catching on anything with a gauze bandage, and then it's off to the cashier to pay the bill. Saline solution, antiseptic wipes, antibiotic, and nursing care $3500 HK (approx. £300) per day.

Anthony and I are going out! This will be the young couple's first time on their own together for some time. We are finally making our long-talked-about trip to The Peak for a spot of tourism. It's a beautifully warm, sunny day as we head for the number 15 bus stop. The bus is the same one that we take to the hospital; only today we are staying on to the end of the line.

The Peak is the highest point on Hong Kong Island and has amazing views that sweep from the skyscrapers of the city, to Victoria Harbour, and to the green hills of the New Territories. This has been the city's most exclusive neighbourhood since colonial times. After a journey that winds its way up the hillside we arrive at the Peak Tower, a wok-shaped tower with viewing terraces on different levels. We have left the sunshine behind and the spectacular views are slightly obscured by mist. There are shops and restaurants, but we settle on taking one of the walks that winds through the hilly landscape. It really is a world away from the hustle and bustle of the city, and just what we need to help us unwind and relax. We mingle with tourists, take photos and buy souvenirs for friends and family, ordinary activities that are very therapeutic. We make the return journey by the world-famous tram, which provides us with a really spectacular view of the city, and literally brings us down to earth, and our nightly duties, rather too quickly.

It is 9 pm and Keso and I are back at Adventist outpatient department for her antibiotic. The nurse has left Keso's two-inch-thick file on the table and she is reading it to pass the time. At 9 pm there is a mix of people in outpatients; some, like us, have come for a treatment appointment, and others arrive as accidents and emergencies. There's a mum carrying her young daughter who has a high temperature, is listless and won't be put down, and needs to be admitted. Her mobile phone is out of battery and she is trying to complete the registration form, pay her deposit, find out when she can speak to the doctor, and get hold of her husband, off the island on business, to let him know what has happened. I lend her my phone as we wait for the cashier to take our payment. 'Good luck,' I say, feeling a bond with her. It doesn't matter that my daughter is twenty-six and hers only four, I fear it's going to be a long night for her.

I could do this trip in my sleep now. The only things that vary are the aircon temperature in the taxi and the level of English spoken by the driver. To deal with the first we carry sweaters and shawls, and for the latter Keso has her address in Cantonese on her iPhone.

I write:

> First follow up with Dr Fan since being discharged. He
> inspects the wounds and is happy with how they are
> healing. He removes the stitches and changes the
> dressings. We also receive the initial results of the blood
> tests, which show continued signs of improvement, but
> we are still waiting for the results from the culture
> samples. We discuss medication, compression leggings
> (the white stockings), and what the future might bring. Dr
> Fan explains the brain's healing process, the risk of
> seizures and the importance of Keppra. Another
> appointment is made for Thursday so that he can inspect
> the wounds again and wash Keso's head.

Once home Keso decides that it is time to unpack her boxes
which have been sitting untouched in the apartment since her re-
admittance to hospital. I take this to be a good sign. This task
requires some negotiation, as Jay has already unpacked and
hung his belongings, and as we women all know, when it comes
to space for our clothes, negotiation and compromise are not easy
concepts!

Jay has an interview for a job…

Our twice-daily hospital visits are going well and getting us all up
early. After the antibiotics Keso has half an hour of physiotherapy
and then its back down the hill for lunch and a siesta. Sometimes
lunch is bought on our way home and sometimes we cook it, but
the kitchen equipment that we have so far been able to purchase
limits our menu. There are also differences in our palates – Keso
and I preferring salads and Jay being a dedicated carnivore.

It's Keso's third day at home, and Anthony and I think an outing in
her neighbourhood would be nice. This afternoon we decide to go
to Victoria Park, for Keso a manageable walk away in Causeway
Bay. I've spent a few afternoons in the park already. It is the

largest public park on Hong Kong Island; it has a fast-food restaurant, an outdoor pool and several kinds of sports facilities, and is a venue for festivals and exhibitions. There are secluded seating areas, trees for shade and beautiful shrubs and flowers. It is a calming green lung in a fast-paced city. Unfortunately, and unknown to us, it is set-up day for the Hong Kong Flower Festival.

The show lasts for nine days and attracts nearly 600,000 visitors. Over two hundred organisations from eighteen countries showcase exotic flowers, landscape and floral art displays, and there are fringe activities including music, dance, green talks, demonstrations and workshops. The theme this year is 'When Blossoms Dance' and the chosen flower is the beautiful orchid, 'Oncidium'. The usual calm of the park has given way to frantic activity, and it is teeming with people. Not the best venue to choose at this time for Keso's re-entry into public life!

As we walk slowly around the park, Keso with her walking stick, bald head and bandage, she is constantly being stared at by couples, individuals and whole families. They make no effort to hide their interest in a tall, foreign girl with no hair, a head wound and a walking stick. It probably only piques their interest more that I am a woman of colour and her father is white. We sit down on a bench to allow Keso to rest and people stand in front of her, looking her up and down, and when they are ready to continue on their way, they walk away from her backwards so as to keep up the inspection for as long as possible. They nudge their walking companions just in case they haven't noticed, and point at Keso. She is furious and close to tears and demands to be taken home. We have a silent, uncomfortable walk to the taxi rank outside of IKEA, and are all much relieved to be heading home. I suspect that this experience has been the trigger to release anger that has been building up in Keso for some time.

Another key factor playing a part in Keso's response is her vision. Dr Fan warned her that after the surgery focusing on extreme left and right would be problematic for a while, particularly as her vision has been limited to an indoor environment for so long. This is her first outing, disorientating enough without the addition of blurred vision affecting her movement. While it seemed like a good idea at the time, this trip has been more overwhelming for her than we could ever have imagined.

In half an hour Keso and her dad will set off for the nightly administration of antibiotics. Tomorrow Dr Fan will wash Keso's head – unheard of, a neurosurgeon moonlighting as a hairdresser! He wants to show me how to do it, as he is emphatic that Keso's hair should be washed every day and kept very short as a precaution against further infections. She will also visit Dr Kay, as he would like to see her before he sets off for the UK. Our Hong Kong days are getting warmer, with humidity around 90/95 per cent.

In my update I recount our experiences in Victoria Park and Keso gets a lot of sympathetic, supportive posts:

> You know what – Keso will always be a head turner. Horrid though if it's just curiosity and not amazement and envy at the beauty...

> Tell Keso to stare ruthlessly back at the starers. That should straighten them out. Although personally, I'd think they'd stare at Keso under any circumstances; she's much too beautiful to go unnoticed...

> You can't help but look at Keso; she's drop dead gorgeous...

An email from Ann reminds me of home:

> It's been marvellous to be kept so up to date with Keso's progress and I thank you for that. However I've started to look forward to the good news and cheery spirits so I

might feel a bit deprived when they stop. The early bulletins were so worrying and unsettling, Lord knows how you all managed that long dark tunnel; by being all together I suppose. I so wish you well and long to see you back and in recovery in London. Spring has sprung here for sure; lovely London is putting on a colourful, green shoots face, so that's definitely something for you to look forward to. My loving feelings with you all, specially that little miracle, brave baby of yours.

I love the spring with its promise of magical things to come! But it also feels a bit spring-like here on another level; the dark days appear to be behind us, and there is a sense of resurrection of life. March 21st is the Spring Equinox, when day and night are equal in length all over the earth, but at this time light is gaining. It is gaining in our lives as well. I believe that the hopes and dreams that brought Keso to Hong Kong are now within her reach.

As if to mark this new awareness, I decide it is time to reduce our daily update to every other day. I write:

Keso is settling back into life in Wan Chai. While our trip to Victoria Park didn't go so well, she and Jay walked to the bank today and then on to Marks & Spencer to get their supper – fish and chips. Stepping into M&S, a familiar British institution here in Hong Kong, is a disturbing experience. The layout and items are just what you would find in any M&S on any high street in the UK. The only difference in products that I find is in the dressings that accompany the ready-made salads; they are clearly made for a Hong Kong palate. Keso is taking work calls and is beginning cautiously to think about when and what she might be able to do from home when she's feeling up to it.

Anthony and I have some more time off, a sure sign that Keso is on the mend. We take the bus to Repulse Bay on the southern side of the island, a beautiful crescent-shaped stretch of sand with designer shops, award-winning restaurants, picturesque gardens leading down to the beach, and a beautifully calming view out to sea. It's an upmarket residential area, but with a relaxed, resort-like feel to it. I have no swimsuit and anyway I can't swim, but Anthony, who can never resist the sea, strips down to his underpants and goes in for a swim. For me it is enough to lie in the sunshine and listen to the waves. There is no one else venturing into the water, it is only March, but there are a few tourists with cameras on the beach taking the obligatory selfie, and posed shots of each other. In this part of the world sunbathing is not the same 'must do' activity that it is in the West, particularly among women. All across Asia a fair complexion is highly prized. A young woman lies on the sand nearby, carefully positioning herself for a selfie. She is wearing leggings, a long-sleeved flowing top, a headscarf and a shawl. All that the sun can get at are her hands and eyes.

We go for a walk along the coastline and watch a young boy fly his drone out over the sea. We sit outside the restaurant in the fading sunlight looking out to sea, having a cold beer, and for a brief moment in time the events of the past two months have not intruded. We decide to buy a treat for Keso and Jay, and settle on a serving of apple crumble and custard each, beautifully packaged for the journey. On our walk back to the bus stop we encounter a coach load of Chinese tourists – 'mainlanders' as they are more locally known here – and I once more become the object of curiosity and scrutiny. A familiar experience, but one I never get used to or feel comfortable with. We catch the bus and begin the ascent and descent as it winds its way around the Peak back to the hustle and bustle of Wan Chai. To be a bus ride away from the beach is a new experience for me, and one I could happily get used to. As the sun fades from sight our beautiful day comes to an end.

The following day, maintaining the illusion of being tourists, we head for the Hong Kong Heritage Museum in the New Territories.

This is the area between Kowloon and Mainland China. This time the journey is made by MTR, the ever-expanding Mass Transit Railway that rapidly transports you underground around the island and further afield. It is well maintained and comfortable, being air-conditioned all year round, and efficient and highly affordable, with the average journey being $4.4 HK – about 35p. Unlike in the UK there is also Wifi connection! We each have our Octopus cards, purchased for us by Jess on our arrival in Hong Kong, and they operate much like our Oyster card in London.

The museum is built in the tradition of *si he yuan,* to resemble a compound of houses around a central courtyard. It is simple, natural and beautiful. There are several galleries, but unfortunately for us they are almost all closed for refurbishment and the creation of a new exhibition. The Bruce Lee exhibition is the only one open; it has over 600 items of memorabilia and is surprisingly interesting, with insights into his family life and philosophy of martial arts.

After our visit we take the train to Prince Edward Station to visit the fish market. Whatever I am expecting it is not this. The street is lined on either side with shops selling fish as pets, and fish paraphernalia of every kind. What our guidebook failed to tell us is that most of the fish are displayed in tightly tied plastic bags, containing very little water and often too small for the fish. Fish aquariums in this part of the world are believed to bring luck – but clearly not for the fish!

Our last stop is the flower market. My feet won't take much more and I'm getting tired and hungry, so we take a quick stroll up and down the shop front displays of beautiful flowers – a soothing sight after the fish experience. We end our outing rather sadly in a McDonalds; it's all we can find on the busy main road and we are too tired to search any further. Anthony orders something but I decide to wait until we get home. Tomorrow we're on Keso duty while Jay has a World Instagram meet-up with a group of photographers here in Hong Kong.

The emails continue; God bless social media! I hear from Karen:

> *Dearest Joan, I don't always reply to your emails but I wanted you to know that I love your daily updates and so many people are asking after you all. Your energy is spreading far and wide... Love and hugs. I reply: Dear Karen it's 7 minutes past midnight here – what lovely words to fall to sleep with! I always sense your presence Karen... Love and hugs back to you.*

I write to Julia for more support now we are back in Wan Chai:

> *Keso's veins are becoming rather sore because of the powerful antibiotics being administered twice a day, and I wondered if you might have a suggestion for how we might address this. Your recommendations have been such a help to us. We have discovered the Integrated Medical Institute here in Hong Kong and plan to have a conversation with them in the near future.*

Julia replies:

> *Keso's recovery and her positive mindset continue to be remarkable through all the challenges! Her poor veins – it's little wonder they're feeling irritated. There are 2 options to soothe them; the first approach would be homeopathic. Ledum 30c addresses bruising, soreness and pain from the IV – it is specific for puncture wounds. Ledum acts deeper than arnica and it is amazing for IV issues. In addition you can use a topical homeopathic cream around the IV site. They come in arnica, arnica/calendula, or arnica/hypericum, (hypericum is great for nerve pain). If you don't want to go the homeopathic route, you can use essential oils. Lavender is always good and covers all bases – burning, swelling, soreness and bruising. Also try the peppermint, which is very soothing and helps with bruising. How fabulous about the Integrated Medical Institute! They'll be such a*

*good source and support for you. I'm so happy for you all
to be back at Keso and Jay's. The hospital environment is
so surreal and weirdly detaches you from yourself doesn't
it? I hope one of the suggestions brings rapid relief...*

Dr Fan has requested that I come with Keso on her next
appointment so that I can observe the hair-washing technique, as
this is now being handed over to me back in the apartment. I am
still in awe of a neurosurgeon washing my daughter's slowly
regrowing hair! We are led into a large examination room where
Keso is instructed to lie on the couch. A nurse fills a shaped bowl
with warm water on Dr Fan's instruction. Dr Fan removes his
charcoal grey cashmere sweater, and rolls up the sleeves of his
white shirt. He takes something that resembles my washing-up
sponge-scourer from a sealed packet and immerses it in water. It
foams up when saturated. With Keso lying on the table and the
shaped washing bowl fitted around her neck, he proceeds to scrub
her head, first with the scourer – over and around the sites – and
then with the sponge. He gradually takes in all of her head,
scrubbing firmly for some time. All the time emphasising how
important it is for us to keep the scalp clean and to wash her hair
everyday, he repeats that she must keep it short to avoid the
possibility of another infection. I ask if I can buy these sponges
and he gives me the one he has been using. They are hospital
stock and have to be accounted for, and he doesn't know if I can
get them elsewhere. Confident that I now have the required hair-
washing skills, we head home.

Keso sends her first update:

*Thank you. These are two words I've said a lot recently.
To nurses, doctors, my family; even to my own limbs as
they begin to work again. It's also something that I need
to say to many of you. To all those who sent me
messages of support and love, who shared my story, to
those who I've met and those I'm yet to meet – thank you
for everything. Your messages and prayers have kept me*

going, made me smile, given me strength and reminded me that there is goodness and joy in this world when I was at my lowest. You have all been truly incredible and I will remember the support you have given me for the rest of my life.

It is accompanied by a photograph of Keso with her now short hair, holding the 'Thank You' banner that she wrote herself.

It's the weekend and the four of us are out for our very first Hong Kong Sunday lunch together. After lunch we step back in time and take a trip the entire length of the island, on one of Hong Kong's historic trams, from Causeway Bay to Kennedy Town. The trams have been around since 1904 and are incredibly cheap – each tram ride costs a flat fare of $2.30 HK (18p) no matter how far you travel. We have the best view and the most air next to a window on the upper deck. They are not the most comfortable form of transport, with small wooden seats and little or no suspension, but they are environmentally friendly and slow enough for us to take in the sights and get some great photos. We end our trip with a glass of wine in the Bulldog Bar overlooking the sea at Kennedy Town; fruit juice for Keso, as Dr Fan says no alcohol at the moment.

On our tram ride we are able to have a good view of one of Hong Kong's less celebrated 'institutions'. Every Sunday thousands of female workers from Indonesia and the Philippines gather together across Hong Kong. Most are employed as maids and carers for the city's wealthy families. Under government regulations they must be given twelve consecutive hours of free time each Sunday. Since the women have no accommodation of their own, being required by law to live in their employers' home, on their day off they gather on Hong Kong's walkways, in parks and outside public buildings to eat, dance, relax and socialise.

Keso had her last stitch out this morning and Dr Fan is pleased with her progress, although he is pushing her to do more physiotherapy and to start doing some work. He's all about how far she has to go rather than how far she's come. I send a video together with a brief update: *Keso is dancing and may finally have regained her black woman 'riddim'!*

Jay attends another interview for the same job at Quarry Bay...

Reflections:
I sit quietly in the Silence listening to my breathing, giving thanks for where we are on the journey back to full health. I read another synchronous post on Facebook, this time from Wayne Dyer:

> *Be aware of your own amazing capacity to affect the*
> *healing and health of those around you simply by the*
> *silent presence of your connection to intention.*

These words bring me great joy. I have been doing what feels right moment-to-moment; I tell myself that there is no blueprint that I am following, just my instinct. But when I read Wayne Dyer's words I realise that there is and always has been a blueprint. It is my belief that we live in a Universe of Infinite Intelligence, that this Power permeates everything, that we are all an expression of this Power which is a Power for Good, that we can use it in our lives on a mental level by means of our thoughts, beliefs and words. Fenwicke Holmes says that it is 'the method by which spirit passes into manifestation... [and] through it, it shall be done unto you according to your faith...' This is part of what I have spent four years learning intellectually; now I have been given the opportunity to experience it.

On March 24th I write:

> *A sad day today, Anthony left us for the UK. Last night*
> *Team Keso (Hong Kong branch) had a farewell meal*
> *together at Le Relais de l'Entrecôte in Wan Chai. A lovely*

French steak restaurant, serving only steak and chips. They serve you half your enormous portion of steak and chips at the first serving and keep the other half warm for you for your second helping, an interesting experience. We had a great evening, and we are all sorry to see Anthony leave us. We have been such a strong team and Anthony's departure reminds us that soon Team Keso will be redundant and life will change once again – we are both happy and sad.

6 – ALL CHANGE

Life is a series of natural and spontaneous changes.
Don't resist them; that only creates sorrow.
Let things flow naturally forward in whatever way they like.
Lao Tzu

It is the end of March and I have been in Hong Kong for two months now, and know that some day soon I shall not be needed as close by as I have been during these shocking weeks. I am making the most of my time with my daughter and hopeful of seeing more of Hong Kong before I have to leave.

On his departure Anthony hands over control of the envelope stuffed full of crisp new $500 HK bills, on which we have been drawing for our day-to-day expenses. This is what we will use to pay for the daily hospital visits and our day-to-day living costs. It seems like an awful lot of money but we don't have to spend it all, and anyway I shall probably be gone before the money is. It sits in a box file on Jay's desk, and at first I am tentative about taking anything and rigorous about keeping a record. It seems slightly decadent to have this much money lying around and to be able to help myself to it so freely, when we have been so preoccupied with our thoughts and fears around lack of this precious resource.

But then quite suddenly I am used to it, and no longer feel any guilt at dipping into the envelope; I trust myself and the universe's ability to replenish! I have never questioned the values I hold about money, but I find that I am suddenly acquiring new ones that feel much more my own and much more comfortable; and am letting go of those that I now see I inherited rather than chose for myself. Ernest Holmes wrote: 'There is a continuous movement toward me of supply, of money, of all that I need to express the fullest life, happiness and action.'

Julia writes:

> I am so sorry that Anthony had to leave, but what blissful circumstances he was able to depart under. Keso's progress is nothing short of staggering and that you were all able to go out on an extended excursion must have brought enormous joy. I have a very strong feeling Keso is going to continue to make giant strides – and hops and leaps and pirouettes. The dancing video was outrageous! Keso is so lucky to have you there to wrap her in constant support and comfort and encouragement, the best healing we have to offer and receive. May the miracles continue!

Our daily Adventist visits continue, but Keso's veins are rebelling. I think the word has got around about the 'intruder' antibiotic and the veins have closed ranks in an act of solidarity. Keso's mind knows the score with the antibiotics, but her heart has joined the protesters and there's a battle underway. They've had to change site twice in the last two days and not without causing her some pain. The veins are hiding and the nurses are stabbing in the dark at everything that looks even vaguely possible. We are all dreading the clock hands pointing to nine, and the tension on the taxi ride must be akin to that in a game of Russian roulette. We are hoping that Dr Fan will consider putting her on oral antibiotics now as she's been on the IV for four weeks.

We had a shopping trip together today and it was a lovely distraction. We are planning a trip to Kowloon, to stroll around Ladies Market; her physiotherapist says she should walk more. Keso's most recent success, however, has been 'mistressing' escalators again, and this gets a big thumbs-up from her! She gets a great deal of practice on Central's and Mid-Levels' escalator and walkway system. It is the longest outdoor covered escalator system in the world. Hong Kong is dominated by steep, hilly terrain and so it was built in 1993 to provide a better commute by linking areas within the Central and Western Districts on the island. It consists of twenty escalators and three inclined moving walkways – and is a great tourist attraction!

At the end of her tether, Keso contacts Dr Fan about the IV situation and to ask about changing to oral antibiotics. Dr Fan suggests the PICC – Peripherally Inserted Central Catheter, which cousin Angela also suggested some time ago when it met with the thumbs-down from Keso. Dr Chan, the neuro-anaesthesiologist recommended by Dr Fan, talks us through this option, but is not in favour of it. He says the risk of infection is greater if it isn't managed on an inpatient basis in the more sterile environment of a ward, with nurses trained to administer it. Dr Chan inspects Keso's arms and declares that she has 'good veins'; he offers to insert the IV himself using a local anaesthetic to deal with the pain Keso is beginning to experience. The nurse preps the site with the local anaesthetic cream an hour before the IV is inserted. This is then covered with a thin transparent adhesive film to keep it in place while it numbs the area.

On these regular hospital runs my companion of choice these days is my iPhone. Once upon a time it would have been a book, but the circumstances mean that I am unable to concentrate for long periods. Books are a great adventure in themselves, full of highs and lows, evoking a range of emotions, opening a door in the imagination to adventure, the unknown and the unfamiliar. I already have this – and so it's the iPhone, tailor-made for flitting like a butterfly – or rather *surfing* – for easily digestible sound bites of information, for the latest gossip on the street and for sending my updates. This is just about all I can manage at the moment. Both Keso and I occupy ourselves on our respective iPhones until Dr Chan arrives at 10 pm and places the new slim-line IV with no problem. Looking very pleased with himself, he bids us goodbye, slings his jacket over his shoulder and with a smile and a thank-you to the nurse, he is on his way. Another doctor who hasn't charged for his services even though this is his second visit to the hospital today to see Keso.

I receive an email from Wendy, a good friend and cab driver to Anthony on his return to Heathrow:

> *Let's hope the challenging veins were only a minor hiccup in an otherwise positive trajectory towards recovery. Thanks for the bag – so Chinese – it brings back lots of memories of Hong Kong and other parts of China. I don't know how you managed to find the time or headspace to think of me. It was good to see Anthony and feel a bit more in touch – you must be missing him...*

The weather is changing; spring is definitely in the air, as are blossoms on the trees that line some of Hong Kong's streets. Keso has another two weeks of IV antibiotics and so we are still a little apprehensive with each visit, willing her veins to hold out just a little while longer. Keso throws herself into a frenzy of spring-cleaning, mopping, dusting, rearranging, and only meeting resistance when she tries to throw out some of the boxes Jay has been keeping from his latest electronic purchases. Keso is determined to keep the minimalist status of their white-walled apartment, but is having to negotiate the 'how' with Jay. Today he offers to do the evening hospital run with Keso; usually my call, and I curl up on the sofa with a glass of wine, a bowl of crisps and a Morgan Freeman feel-good movie. Yummy!

On the last day of March, to mark the change I feel is upon us, I send an update:

As we said goodbye to Keso and Jay at Heathrow airport last December 23rd, we never could have imagined the shocking twists and turns that Keso's life was soon to take, that would bring us both to Hong Kong. You have all been party to her incredible journey and the highs and lows of her treatment and recovery. We couldn't have got this far without you all. Your amazing words of encouragement, your love and steadfast support have kept us going, particularly through those moments of overwhelming tiredness and uncertainty. All we had to do was open an email or look on Facebook to know that we weren't alone and that we could face the next challenge. The journey is not over for Keso as yet, but we have reached the point from which we can see both how far we have come and how far she has to go. So from this optimistic vantage point we would like to say a heartfelt 'thank you'. Hopefully we will have the opportunity to thank you personally, but in case we don't meet for a while we wanted to say it now. You are awesome people with such big hearts and we love you all!

It's Thursday evening in a busy outpatients department and Keso is just about to be hooked up to her IV. This morning Dr Fan examined the scalp abscess again and decided that it needed aspirating once more, as he could feel that liquid had gathered there again. This time there was no pain as he had administered a large local anaesthetic. Once more her head was tightly bound to encourage the two surfaces to adhere to each other, so that there is no space in which liquid can collect. Jay has taken over from Dr Fan as Keso's hairdresser, and this afternoon she was back in the barber's chair, scissors and clippers at the ready. Short hair really suits Keso and is so much easier for her to manage. For the moment she is satisfied with Jay's efforts; her main focus is still on her recovery and the switch to oral antibiotics. It will be another benchmark on her journey back to full health, when vanity rears its beautiful head and recovery has a rival! I expect that she has already identified the most stylish salons on the island.

With the balmy spring weather and Keso growing stronger, we are able to get out and about. Keso and I go for a walk in the old neighbourhood of Sheung Wan – what I think of as the Montmartre of Hong Kong, and described as *shabby colonial chic, exotic and hip.* There is an elegance to the neighbourhood, which is owed to the mix of old and new – providing a flavour of old Hong Kong. We visit Man Mo Temple, the oldest temple in Hong Kong, built around 1842 as a tribute to the God of Literature (Man) and the God of Martial Arts (Mo), worshipped by students hoping to do well in the civil service of Imperial China. Giant incense coils hang from its ceiling, creating a smoky, intoxicating atmosphere. There are local people worshipping, tourists taking photos and temple workers going about their daily tasks. In their shop I purchase two key rings for Anthony and me, supposedly inscribed with our names in Chinese characters. We stroll down Hollywood Road where I stand in awe of the ancient Banyan trees, whose networks of powerful roots grow out of the stonework, covering the walls and providing a dense canopy of 'dreadlocks' for passers-by, as the trees themselves tower skywards. I am on my second weaving – a triptych inspired by these Banyans – and Keso waits patiently while I take photographs of the trees – they are truly magnificent. We buy drinks and take them into the nearby park where we FaceTime Anthony, bringing him up to date with recent events. He knows that Keso and Dr Fan are still in negotiations about when she can stop the IV and go onto oral antibiotics; we're not sure who will win, so we place no bets.

Keso and I at last make it to Ladies Market in Kowloon. London is getting closer and there are presents to buy. The Ladies Market on Tung Choi Street provides a kilometre stretch of over one hundred stalls of bargain clothing, accessories and souvenirs, and I am keen to put my haggling skills to the test. It feels strange to be doing this when I am not on holiday, but never one to shirk a shopping trip, I diligently work my way through my list with Keso at my side, offering advice, watching me bargain with stall holders and chivvying me along. She's getting tired. While the 'tsunami' has passed there are still little eddies of turbulence from time to time that threaten to unbalance Keso. But there are golden moments for mother and daughter to share together that do so much to support her recovery – and mine.

I write:

> Out in the sunshine today! Ending up at Lab Made again for our instant nitrogen-frozen ice creams – delicious flavours. Then it's home for a rest before tonight's hospital visit. Keso's new site is working well and we have high hopes that it will be good for several more doses... There's not much sign of Easter here, no displays of Easter Eggs or fluffy yellow chicks in shop windows to remind us of this Christian festival. Keso and Jay go to an afternoon viewing of 'Fast and Furious' at the cinema with friends, so that Cinderella-like she can be back at the hospital before the clock strikes 9. On Dr Chan's suggestion, Keso is now taking her antibiotics lying down listening to music. I don't know why we didn't think of this earlier, it means that she is relaxed, and so hopefully are her veins.

Dr Fan is with us this evening to remove the stitch, see how 'the lump' is doing after its aspiration, and to get the results of the blood test. Some liquid has collected, but the blood test shows that it is clear of infection. However, he will only agree to oral medication when the site is empty, and the inflammatory markers have normalised. He tells her that clinically she is doing well, but he wants to be reassured about her cognitive development and says that her manager would be the best assessor of this, so wants her to start working from home. We always come away from Dr Fan feeling a little dissatisfied and – in Keso's case – angry, because he can't as yet give us what we desperately want: a clean bill of health. I sense myself getting frustrated with Keso's anger and frustration, and recognise this as a sign of my tiredness. At moments like this I know it is best to say nothing and so I keep silent and walk. What is in no doubt is that Keso is making steady progress.

Another email from Ann:

> *Darling Joan, will you come and be my mum (when Keso is better of course)? It must be wonderful to have you by one's side at such a time and Keso's recovery must have been enhanced and expedited by having you there. When you get home we will give you LOTS of infusions (by mouth) of all kinds so that your recovery from this long trial is short and sweet. Easter was short and chocolate sweet and tomorrow its all back to normal. London is good when everyone is either in bed or in the country. It's so quiet and peaceful and this year incredibly sunny and warm. I've just been planting my window boxes and will get into the garden, which is much neglected, this coming week I vow – I'm a bit of a fair weather gardener.*

I have no idea if Ann knows how nourishing and healing her emails are for me. They push the button that releases all my pent up emotions. I am cared for; someone knows how devastated and exhausted I feel. I write:

> *Dearest Ann, I cried and laughed on reading your email. Words of kindness and recognition touch my soul and remind me how blessed and supported I am. You are right; London is a beautiful place when we get out of its way – especially when long-awaited Spring arrives. I so look forward to the treats in store for me! Chocolate is on the list. I think I will have a great challenge in the garden. Antoine (Anthony) is good for mowing and hacking off tree limbs, but the beds need a lighter touch. Please come to France with us again…*

Our days in Wan Chai settle into a comfortable rhythm: early rising, hospital, exercises for Keso, weaving for me, siesta for Keso while I walk, outing, supper, hospital, bed.

My services are still required for the daily shower. Jay has bought a folding chair from IKEA, which just fits the shower cubicle. Hair-wash comes first. Luckily Keso's shower has two showerheads – the large, fixed overhead rosette, and the hand-held hose, which is ideal for hair-washing. I fill a bowl with warm water from the hose, pour it over Keso's head and then, using the scouring pad, lather her head. I have become more confident in my work and apply a good pressure, mindful of Dr Fan's concerns about hair hygiene. A couple more bowls full of water to rinse and the shampoo is gone. Then I turn my attention to soaping Keso's body, after which it's the overhead spray, and I can leave Keso to enjoy it on her own. During shower time Keso has me telling her stories of her childhood. I am surprised at the things that I remember – dancing her to sleep on summer nights in France to the music of Earl Klugh; threatening to smack her on a picnic on the Ile d'Oleron, because she was tearing the wrappers off the Laughing Cow cheese squares; the day a wasp flew into and out of her mouth while she was drinking a coke. I am exhausted; it's late in the day, her cannula needs sealing in a plastic bag, the bathroom is small and steamy, there is a lot of Keso to oil and to dry, and she still needs help lifting her left leg into and out of the shower. But I enjoy this unique time together; we shall not see its like again. I remember little of the joys of bath time in her childhood. I expect that I was always in a hurry. This opportunity for conscious mothering is precious to me.

I write:

> It's a grey day here in Hong Kong. We were threatened
> with a typhoon that never happened. I am disappointed; I
> was looking forward to the experience, especially as it
> was only a number 1. Once it gets to a number 3 and

above offices are closed and people have to stay inside…
Next week is a busy one, MRI scan, blood tests and
appointment with Dr Fan. Finally we will know when Keso
can start taking her antibiotics orally.

Keso has been talking to her manager about working from home. She is starting to feel bored and restless, and also worried about her finances. She has not worked since the end of January, and given that she was only three weeks in the job when she was admitted to hospital, the company has been incredibly generous, patient and supportive. They are being sensibly cautious and ask her for a letter from Dr Fan stating that she is fit to begin working from home. He is very happy to comply as he has been urging her to start working for some time. Keso and her manager discuss her return to work and set a minimum of fifteen hours per week paid at an hourly rate based on her salary. It is also agreed that Keso can do more than the fifteen hours if she feels up to it. Keso is happy to be working again: 'It proves that my brain is working OK.' However, it takes time to feel comfortable interacting with the team and clients again.

We receive another four-figure gift of money from a very dear friend, and I write back:

Dear Angela, what an incredibly generous act. Words
always seem inadequate at times like these, but thank
you so very much. Keso's amazing journey of recovery
has been supported by the love and healing energy sent
by friends and family, and by the very practical financial
support which enables her (and us) to stop worrying
about how bills will be paid and get on with the job of
getting better. You have enabled both her peace of mind
and her physical recovery. I can't say it enough times –
thank you!

We've had a bad day. The IV is very slow and the nurses very busy with not enough time to give real thought to Keso's question about whether or not to change the IV site. Tomorrow is the MRI scan and if the veins 'stop working' she won't be able to have the scan, as they won't be able to inject the 'contrast' into her veins. She feels that their advice to keep the site is because they are busy, rather than the best-considered course of action. She's angry and despairing, there are lots of tears and swearing – probably doing her good.

She makes the decision to contact Dr Chan, and he agrees to come tonight and change the site. However, it's difficult to know where to prep for the change because the veins are not easy to see right now – probably hiding from the constant invasion! More anger, tears, and despair. Added to this, Dr Chan says that if Dr Fan wants to continue with IV antibiotics Keso may need to consider the PICC. It has been a difficult day for her. We've had times like this before and come through them, but they knock her back and show how vulnerable she still feels. Despite all this angst, or perhaps because of it and Keso's ability to come through it, the new line is fitted with no problem and it's a much happier Keso who chats to me on the taxi ride home.

I write:

> *Walking along the Bowen Trail to meet Jay and Keso at the hospital where Keso is having her blood test and MRI scan. It is possible to walk from home to the hospital in around an hour. I have two routes – along the busy streets of Wan Chai to the Hopewell Centre, opposite Jess and Edward. Then up to the 17th floor by lift and out onto the hillside on which Hong Kong is built, to follow the beautiful man-made trail up to the hospital, with a breath-taking view of Hong Kong, the harbour and across to Kowloon. The other route starts a few steps from home and takes me onto the elevated walkways that criss-cross Hong Kong. This takes me across busy roads, over public open spaces and through buildings obliged to provide public right of way by the government. This is a great way to see Hong Kong and beat the crowds. This particular*

route also brings me to the lift in Hopewell and up to the Bowen Trail.

It's physio day and Keso is now doing reformer Pilates. Pilates offers amazing core strengthening work, and this is just what Keso needs now. It is the most gentle, safe and effective way to exercise, and the beauty of doing it on the reformer is that you can adjust the level of intensity to suit your own body, using the springs. The reformer looks like a wooden bed with a series of springs and pulleys – where the mattress would be – to create resistance. Pilates is something she used to do regularly in London, and she's enjoying giving her body a workout in a familiar way once more.

We visit with Dr Fan and there is good news – he writes that 'Keso's recovery is remarkable.' In real terms this means that once the current IV site stops working she's off the IV and on to oral antibiotics. And we have the new medication to prove it! Back home to Wan Chai in the sunshine for a celebratory lunch on their section of the elevated walkway, where there are a great many eating-places with tables outside in the sun. We choose a steak house, Jay and I order a juicy steak each and Keso orders fish. Wickedly I have a glass of red and Keso has a white wine spritzer – a delicious way to celebrate the next phase on her road to recovery!

I am still sending a steady stream of thank-you emails. I write to Delcia and the distant healers:

> *We know without a doubt that Keso's amazing recovery could not have been achieved without you all.*
> *Technology and social media have played their part in the healing process, enabling us to stay connected to the love that is always present but that sometimes we doubt.*
> *Facebook and the Internet have been the conduit, but all of you have opened your hearts to us and stayed focused and steadfast when we were tired and struggling. Thank*

you for your love and support, Keso could not have come
so far so quickly without it.

Thursday, April 16th is an historic occasion – Keso comes off the IV and starts taking her antibiotics orally. Such freedom! She has adult privileges again, she can now shower, dry herself and wash her own hair, and she relishes the privacy. Best of all, she no longer has to suffer Jay and me guarding her like G4S security officers when we're out walking. It also means an end to our lives being governed by the 9 am and 9 pm hospital visits. We all have a glorious lie-in to celebrate the change.

Keso is looking at ways to continue getting back in shape. Swimming is off the menu; Dr Fan is worried about the possibility of Keso having a seizure while in the water, and he is also worried about her running until she builds up a bit more stamina. She has decided to join a local gym and use the treadmills.

Keso's arms are finally free, but have taken a battering. They are full of puncture marks and slightly black and blue from the needles, and her veins have hardened. We continue our nightly ritual based on the advice we received from Julia. Before bed I rub Keso's arms with arnica and calendula cream, apply the peppermint oil and impregnate a tissue with the purification oil to help ensure a restful night. We have also taken to watching an episode of *House* on Netflix every night. It is a hospital-based series, strangely comforting, and Keso enjoys being able to say 'I've had that!' to each treatment suggested for the dangerously ill patient by House and his team.

Reflections:
I have come to realise that everything is made brighter, illuminated in the Silence. Those events that have the potential to cause pain and suffering, once brought to the Light have been transformed from threats to opportunities. Looking deeply into my fears rather

than trying to escape them has been the means of transcendence. All through this shocking experience I have sought through faith to move beyond duality to an understanding that unity through love is what heals. In March, in my *Science of Mind* journal on the theme of Mindfulness I read:

> It can be difficult to see the oneness of all life when we look at conditions in society. Duality seems to be everywhere. We view the world from our perspectives of high and low, good and bad, right and wrong and get caught up in appearances, forgetting that behind it all, there is only one... God is all there is... if God is all there is, and God is love, how can these other things possibly exist?... we must learn to transcend appearances of duality and recognise that these experiences are the way we learn on a first-hand basis about the love that God is. It is by going through suffering that we appreciate the relief that comes when we let go of our human opinions and accept life as it comes. We don't appreciate the laughter until we've had the tears, but once we get through the tears, we are more deeply grateful for the laughter.

7 – ZAI HUI

Until we meet again

Update:

> *Yesterday was our appointment with Dr Fan. A happy Dr Fan! He is really pleased with the progress that Keso is making, and the fact that she has experienced no serious side effects. I take the opportunity to thank him for looking after Keso, as I imagine I won't be seeing him again – her next appointment is in a fortnight and my days are numbered. He says, 'Now is the time for you to relax a little, Keso!' and announces that he will be seeing her fortnightly from here on instead of weekly. Life is changing...*

On one of our days out we visit the Integrated Medical Institute (IMI). We like what we see and Keso is advised to book an appointment with Graeme Bradshaw. He is a naturopath and homeopath, and the founder and one of the Directors of the IMI. They have a holistic vision of health underpinned by the principles of Heal, Balance, Evolve, and are committed to achieving 'optimal health and total well-being in mind, body, emotions and spirit'. We are looking forward to our visit. Keso says that she wants me to come. I suggest that she spends time with Graeme on her own, and say that I won't be offended if she decides she doesn't need me at all. However, she is adamant that she wants me to be with her for the appointment. We have a while to wait and this gives us the opportunity to get a feel of the place. There are books to read and buy, and an impressive range of high-end products on sale. Friendly staff come and go, making sure that we are being attended to, and a mother and young child enter the waiting area from one of the treatment rooms, looking happy and relaxed.

Now it is our turn. Graeme comes to find us in the waiting room, introduces himself and ushers us into his room. I am slightly uncomfortable; I don't want him to think that I am an anxious, interfering, overprotective mother who insists on being present. Graeme turns to Keso and asks for her reason for the appointment. Efficiently she paints him a picture of the past three months. He listens, holding eye contact with her, and occasionally making notes. She has his full attention and he doesn't interrupt, only now and then raising his eyebrows as she shares particularly shocking aspects of her story. It is a very useful, thorough session. Graeme acknowledges Keso's story and shows his understanding of the impact it will have had on her health and well-being, and also shows that he has a good grasp of the main issues. He offers Keso advice and suggests supplements to help counteract the adverse effects of all of her medication, and also to help strengthen and rebalance her after such a traumatic experience. He refers briefly to other possible treatments for the future, but suggests that she takes things a step at a time and sees him again in a couple of months. She will need this time to begin to see any improvement in her health, and he also acknowledges that my leaving is bound to have an effect on her.

From their dispensary we collect: omega 3 for brain stimulation, a selection of probiotics to aid digestion (OMX, Optibac and

Reureri), Meriva to help prevent yeast infection, zinc for the immune system and vitamin D to give her system a boost. I take the opportunity to get some vitamin D for myself, after Graeme observes that people of colour living outside of the tropics do not get enough sun to ensure the necessary level of vitamin D.

It's April 18th and my days here now are numbered, and I will soon be redundant. Keso and I are spending as much time as we can doing nice things together. We have a lovely day out at Nan Lian Garden and Chi Lin Nunnery in the New Territories; the weather is beautiful, as are the surroundings. The nunnery is a large temple complex of elegant wooden architecture housing Buddhist relics and peaceful lotus ponds. There is a series of temple halls containing statues representing various divinities and bodhisattvas.

Keso and I wander through the elegant building, stopping to bow to the statues that capture our hearts and our imagination. Nan Lian is a public park built in the style of the Tang dynasty, beautifully landscaped and housing a magnificent collection of bonsai trees. Everything in the garden is arranged according to classical Tang style and rules. It is all a feast for the eye, the spirit and the ear, as soothing music follows us around the temple halls. I leave there wishing that they offered retreats, but knowing that just these few hours have been a restorative. To bring us back down to earth, we round off the day with a sweet treat in an ice-cream parlour in Tin Hau. Keso has milk ice cream with all the trimmings and I have mango and coconut – all topped off with a lovely glass of cold, fresh watermelon juice. Life is good!

Keso, Jay and I are off to visit Big Buddha on Lantau Island. I put my hand in the folder on Jay's desk and discover that I am removing the last $500 bill.

The scary cable car ride over the sea lasts for about half an hour and gives us spectacular, panoramic views in all directions. It is possible to book a place in the glass-bottom cable car, but we are not that adventurous or that crazy. The Po Lin Monastery made it to the world stage when the larger-than-life Tian Tan Buddha (Big Buddha) statue was erected there in 1993. It sits 34 metres high and faces north, looking over the people of China. There are 268 steps that take you up close to this statue of Buddha with his right hand raised in a blessing. The complex is organised rather like a theme park, with activities, shops, restaurants and walks. Just like the photo opportunities on our seaside piers in the UK, Keso, Jay and I poke our heads through holes in painted boards of samurai warriors, damsels in distress and evil emperors. With London drawing closer by the day, I have my shopping list with me on all our outings, and a few more names get crossed off on our visit to Big Buddha.

I have been raising the matter of my return to London with Keso, albeit half-heartedly. My time here in Hong Kong has been extended and intense. Keso and I – in one of our many intimate conversations – agree that while we would not knowingly have chosen the events of the past few months, given that they happened, we wouldn't have missed them for the world. We have grown closer, shared so much, been so truthful with each other, and experienced miracles. We both know that the parting will be difficult and painful.

I have decided to leave it up to Keso to let me know when she is ready to let me go. This is not an abdication of responsibility, but an intuitive decision that recognises her autonomy. Unsurprisingly Anthony is also gently raising the subject of my return. He has been an amazing support, and without him the three months would have been impossible. He has looked after the house, managed our very complicated finances, been available for Tunde and her son Buddy, and most important, together with Tunde and

Buddy, looked after his mother-in-law. I am now needed to help keep the home fires burning.

Anthony emails to let me know that we have been invited to lunch at the sought-after Petersham Nursery Café in Richmond, and asks if there's a chance I might make it. I reply:

> How lovely! Alas I don't think I can do it. I've had May 5th in mind for my return (sorry should have shared this), but yesterday Keso told me very pointedly that Mother's Day is May 10th. I'm going to have the difficult conversation with her this evening and get an agreed date to leave. I thought she'd be happy to let me go and get on with her life, but there are still difficult moments for her. I have at least said that I need to be back for Buddy's birthday party on the 16th, so we shall work backwards from there this evening.

Keso raises the subject with me today, saying that she supposes that we should go on the Cathay Pacific website to look at making a booking. True to her word, after supper we sit in front of her laptop and bring up the site. After Keso's re-admittance to hospital, Jay contacted the airlines to cancel my return booking, and the ticket was left open for us to rebook at a future date, but within six months. This cannot be done online and so Keso telephones to make my reservation. It comes as something of a blow for Keso to discover that rather than the six months we were told, this particular ticket has to be used within three months! We are two days away from its expiry date of May 1st. The decision has been made for us; I am to leave on May 1st!

Time and money have run out on us. We are both in shock; we sit silently side by side on the sofa holding hands, tears in our eyes. This is too sudden; we expected more time to get used to the idea, to plan my departure. But there is no time; we are thrown into very practical action. I will need another suitcase; I have amassed quite a few new possessions over the past three months, and there are the small thank-you gifts and cards from Keso for friends and family back in the UK who have been a part of the extended Team Keso. We pack and we talk of the past and the future, avoiding the painful present. Keso and I talk of the plan for me to return the following February so that we can truly celebrate our birthdays together. I also give her the mini suitcase full of the daily guides I have been compiling for this moment.

Keso and Jay plan my farewell outing. It is to be a surprise. They take me for drinks in the Ozone Bar, at the top of the tallest building in Hong Kong, the eighth-tallest building in the world, and more than twice the height of the Shard. It takes about a minute to ascend by lift to the 118th floor! At 1,608 ft above sea level, it is the highest bar in the world. It is a beautifully clear, sunny day, and I am happy to have this chance to say goodbye to the island and its surrounding environment that has been my home for the past three months. There is an impressive drinks menu to match the view. Jay goes for a simply presented trio of chocolate cocktails. With Ozone having Hong Kong's largest selection of gins, I settle for an unusual aromatic gin, and for Keso, a compromise – a light cider. We are happy and excited. It's difficult not to be in these surroundings, and if any of us are feeling sad, we don't show it or share it. With our feet firmly on the ground after our cocktails, we head for Catch, a fish restaurant in Kennedy Town. Edward joins us for my last supper; unfortunately Jess is away.

My final morning passes in a haze. We're in a taxi on the way to Central, then the airport express and the very familiar trip to the airport. Bags checked and tagged and on their way to the hold, we make the obligatory trip to the shops for those last-minute things that you don't really need. I buy a soft neck cushion for the flight. It is covered in the names of familiar places in Hong Kong, including Wan Chai – it's a memento. Keso and Jay walk me to departures where we hug and kiss and a few tears are shed. I look back once to see Keso waving and then I'm caught up in the necessities of the present moment...

Jay got the job – Chief Facilities Manager for Citibank!

For my final update I write:

Good morning, this is my last update from Hong Kong, as three months to the day I am returning to the UK this afternoon. It has been an incredible three months! Keso is making an amazing recovery and latterly we have had some great days together just enjoying life! I shall be sad to leave her but so happy that she is well and able to begin the life that she and Jay have planned. I have said this once before but I think it bears repeating – while I would not have chosen to experience the events of these past months, given that it was 'thrust upon me', I wouldn't have missed it for the world! I have learnt so much about so much, met some incredible people, received so much love and support and spent premium time with my darling daughter Keso! What a time we've had!

In the words of Arni Schwarzenegger – I'll be back!!

EPILOGUE

I leave Hong Kong as suddenly as I arrived, no lengthy farewells, no post-mortems. In London I step just as swiftly into the patterns of everyday life. Early morning trips to the gym with Anthony, our Friday shop at Sainsbury, my 5Rhythms dance group on a Saturday morning, my daily early morning walks, time with my grandson Buddy, looking after my ninety-year-old mother. I am swallowed whole back into life in London.

We go to France at the end of May – Anthony, my mother, Tunde, Buddy and I. We spend days working in the garden in glorious sunshine. Tunde starts work on her bottle-top mosaic under our enormous bay tree. We go to Friday market in Riberac and lunch in the Colonnes with friends. I visit Perigueux, capital of the Dordogne, and walk its cobbled streets and along the river with Tunde and Buddy. We swim and paddle in Lac Jumaye. It is so hot that we lift mum in her beach chair into the water so that she can paddle too. We have leisurely evening meals sitting on our terrace watching the pink and purple hues of sunset splash across the horizon. On the surface nothing has changed. But to those who probe I remark that it has been a life-changing experience. In the healing group Nigel asks me in what way, but I have no answer for him. My interior landscape has changed forever in subtle but fundamental ways that are slowly unfolding, but they are part of a lifetime's journey and outside of that context not easy to share, even with those who know something of the voyage.

As I am to have no more recovery time than this, I need to look after myself in other ways. I make an appointment with my osteopath Carol; I know my body has taken on unhealthy postures in my fight to hold things together, and now is the time to let go and show my body some tenderness. Carol tells me that I am exhibiting the classic 'heroic posture'; head up, chin thrust forward, shoulders back, spine straight – *I-must-soldier-on-at-all-costs.* I know this is not just about events in Hong Kong. Looking after my mother, as we have been for the past five years, shapes our days and can be testing. I visit my homeopath Sarah; this tight feeling in my chest, my problems digesting and processing food, all I know stress-related, and needing attention now that the trauma is behind me. I am back in the healing group with space for me. I return to the gym twice a week, and return to my exercises in the pool. I have a long session with Lynne, my metaphysics teacher, to 'find the gift' and take the learning from the journey. With Karen, my coach and now my friend, I discuss my need to write. She is my birthing partner through the coming months, listening, asking questions; like a doula, she takes care of me so that I can give birth to the book. I so look forward to my fortnightly 'check-ups' with her.

Summer approaches and I feel the need to write with some urgency. I have spoken about this with Keso and I have her blessing. There will be others undertaking similar journeys into the unknown, and maybe through my writing I can be a companion to them in their challenging times. I have one glorious week in Puyssonier with Anthony before I return to London and caring for my mother. Tunde and Buddy leave for the summer in France and

I settle down to write. There is trauma, stress and tiredness in my system, and I have my mother, but I find a rhythm and a routine that enable the words to flow. Keso's story, with its destination of perfect health, spills across the pages as I live it once more, but this time secure in the knowledge of the outcome and therefore able to describe and reflect on the process...

It is autumn and I sit in the conservatory of our home in London, looking out at the neat and tidy garden – shrubs and trees relieved of their dead wood, beds weeded, perennials staked and tied, leaves raked – put to bed for the winter. On the page a similar process is at work; I have pruned and cut back, dead-headed, weeded and thinned out so as not to obscure or overshadow what needs to be heard. But however briefly, I feel the need to locate Keso's story within the bigger narrative, where our journey with its exterior and interior destinations really started, seven generations back...

All my life
Ancestral voices have been calling me
In childhood and adolescence ignored
Too busy learning survival skills
Likewise in young adulthood
A time for exploring and enjoying my material world

But then in motherhood
Familiar now with the womb of life
Their collective voices pushing through the day to day
I felt their hands in the small of my back
Seven generations of my line

Their determination became mine
With no idea of where they would take me
But feeling the urgency in those hands
I surrendered

And the journey began...

Doesn't everyone at sometime in their lives hear the voices, feel the hands, becomes aware of something calling? And don't we respond to it in one of three ways: make the decision to answer it and to plunge into unknown realms; ignore it – this is simply a journey I don't want to take; respond by taking the material road well travelled, and make more familiar changes such as move abroad, retrain, start a business.

Each of us makes our choice...

This story also belongs to those ancestral mothers and daughters whose voices echoed through the ages, and whose pleas I finally heeded; it is their longing to be set free that I have heard all my life...

There is a wound in our family
Carefully nurtured and handed down
Mother to daughter

This wound glories in the name of abandonment
Tended and protected by each generation
This ancestral gift has been our karmic inheritance

We know the stories of desertion
Have often heard them told
By grandmother sister aunt

Each of us chooses a favourite
To nourish and preserve
Living our lives around its core

The one who runs away...
The one who keeps the peace...

The one who confronts...

Our own lives abandoned in favour of the wound

But waking up is good for dispelling myths
For recognising them for what they are
Our sacred teachers –
If we are not afraid to learn

It is said most wisely that
'The wound is the place where the Light enters'
And in this moment bathed in the Light of Truth
I know these ancestral tales for what they are

I embrace them as my sages
Thank them for being our companions
And release them to the Light...

Those hands in the small of my back pushed me in many therapeutic directions, delivering me to the doors of great teachers. With each one came the opportunity to heal another chapter in the ancestral story.

There is a death within the pages of this narrative of life, love, faith and resurrection. It is the welcomed death of the stories that limit, restrict and constrain the living. This journey with the ancestors is at an end; I am back at the beginning in the astrological 4th House, the foundation on which everything else rests, often called the House of the end and the beginning of life. Where transformation occurs and life is renewed...

A final gentle tug
And the gate swings open
Fresh air rushes in
Filling spaces left unoccupied for lifetimes...

A light released
Shines clear and bright from within
Illuminating the landscape
And everything looks sounds feels more alive

Apparently there are songs to be sung from this place
Words and ways to be woven
A language of the soul ancient and timeless
To be resurrected...

My time has come
Stepping out of the bardo
I carry the Light with me
And the cloth I have been weaving in eternity
Tumbles out around me...

When peace like a river attendeth my way
When sorrow like sea billows roll
Whatever my lot, Thou hast taught me to say
It is well, it is well with my soul...

Horatio Spafford

AFTERWORD

It is November 2015, and my ticket to Hong Kong on Cathay Pacific is booked for February 4th, almost a year to the day since my first visit. Since her arrival in Hong Kong Keso had been eager for me to visit and for us to celebrate our birthdays together. My answer was always, 'I'd love to, my darling, but what do I do about gran-gran?' As fate would have it, her wish came true, but there were more pressing matters than birthdays that claimed our attention. And so, as I promised when I left seven months ago, I am returning for the celebration we never got to have and to spend time with my daughter, being introduced to the place she now calls home in the way she had planned.

I had imagined also, at the start of writing this tale, that the visit would be needed for closure, but as the story unfolded more and more of itself across the pages, I realised that rather than being a conclusion, it is to celebrate and mark an opening. My reflections in the Silence have been a tool for recognising and opening to my True Self…

Like a celebrity
About to cut the ribbon
I stand joyful
Embracing the peace
As I step into the emptiness…
It is in this opening

That I am to be found
This personality Joan
Still lives and breathes
But someday will cease to be
What if I die before I die?
By which I mean
Mind melts and merges
With the Infinite Self…

Going no where
Content with now here

A WORD ABOUT GOD

I have used the term God in places throughout this book to refer to what many, myself included, believe to be the Life-Giving Impulse in the universe: *the Builder of all forms and the Dweller in each.* Being the Substance of all forms, God is infinite, eternal, and changeless, unknowable by the mind and therefore impossible to explain. But nevertheless this ego has to try!

God is the idea I grew up with in a Christian society, and a Church of England school. My family did not go to church except for weddings and funerals, and only used the terms God and Christ in moments of great frustration and anger. My image of God, when I thought about him, was of an old, white man with long hair and a long beard, stern and paternalistic in outlook, but ultimately fair – if you obeyed his law as taught by church and school – and really only attainable through death.

When, as I grew, I was able to think for myself more clearly, I rejected this anthropomorphised being on an intellectual level, but could not shake him from my psyche. I was caught in the trap of duality, where notions such as good and evil, right and wrong, deserving and undeserving, had me firmly in their grip. This God had me on a seesaw, up one moment and down the next; my life was an emotional roller coaster. I longed for peace, and freedom from the judgement and guilt that came with this image of God.

I finally made the decision to stop denying God and start seeking to understand It. Many journeys later, and with a great deal of pain and suffering endured, I now know God as mother, father, friend, confidante, silence, presence, grace, loving compassion, the peace that passes all understanding, and much, much more... Beyond duality, beyond description, beyond belief...

I do believe that our earthly journey – should we choose to take it – is to find our way back to our essential self, which knows Itself to be part of this Originating, Pure Consciousness...

> For me, God is both personal and impersonal, is and is not, and beyond any of those ideas. He is there, naturally, when the mood inside me yearns for him as God. Then I enjoy him as father, friend, presence, grace, mystical knowledge, benevolence and compassionate love. Otherwise he is not: meaning he is merged in my consciousness as pure, quality-less Being...
>
> Mooji

> Spirituality is natural goodness. God is not a person, God is a presence personified in us. Spirituality is not a thing; it is the atmosphere of God's Presence, goodness, truth and beauty.
>
> Ernest Holmes

POSTSCRIPT

I arrive back in Hong Kong on a beautiful, clear blue, sunny February day. As the plane begins its descent into Lantau Island I keep expecting the cloud cover to appear – Keso had said they'd been having cloudy weather – but it doesn't.

Leaving the plane, I merge with the other travellers, many of whom have arrived to join family and friends in the Chinese New Year (CNY) celebrations. I wheel my trolley slowly through the customs hall and out into arrivals, savouring every moment of being back here under such different circumstances. I am greeted by a stylish, beautiful, beaming young woman holding a sign that reads 'Mumma Kendall!' I beam back. Several hugs and kisses later we head to the juice bar for a well-remembered ginger pick-me-up, and more beaming at each other, we are both so pleased!

Then it's onto the Hong Kong express, and we're heading for Hong Kong Island. This time I am interested in my surroundings, in the new buildings going up, the river traffic and the countryside. I search hungrily for the familiar, and for the changes that are inevitable in such an ever-expanding country. Tsing Yi, Kowloon,

Hong Kong – I watch the strip on the live board of the train light up as we pass each stop. I beam with delight and sigh contentedly, reminding myself that this time I am here to enjoy it all with Keso – on holiday!

We wheel my bags to the orderly line for the familiar red taxi, and wait our turn. In a short time we are back home on Jaffe Road, unloading suitcases. At first glance nothing appears to have changed, except the code to enter the building. The entrance hall is decorated with miniature orange plants, a symbol of good luck and prosperity – the round fruit said to resemble gold coins. Paper decorations in red adorn the walls, all playing their part in welcoming in the coming Year of the Monkey on February 8th, the day before Keso's birthday.

Over a cup of green tea there are updates from me on Anthony, gran-gran, Tunde and Buddy; and on Jay, Jess and Edward from Keso. I shall see Jess tomorrow but Edward leaves for Miami this evening, so it will be a while before we meet. In the apartment there are a few additions. Personal items have appeared on the walls and surfaces of storage units: reminders of family, friends and special events back in the UK. This is now a home with evidence of its occupiers and their personalities and interests, rather than the impersonal (but lovely) white space I had occupied this time last year.

I unpack, amazed at how my things are absorbed into the small apartment. A wonderful much-needed shower and then it's out to do a bit of shopping, before meeting Jay for a drink and supper. On our way out I notice that a whole new building is going up across the road from them! Keso tells me that her metamorphosis into her dad is almost complete – she has Jay asking each day, 'What's the plan?' This was Keso's question from childhood, trained by a father with a love of organising and forward-planning. So in true father-and-daughter fashion I am given the plan for the evening and the following day. I am relieved to see that she has inherited some of my traits, and left a few spaces for the spontaneous.

We are shopping for a small orange plant for the apartment, and so it's a trip to Wan Chai market to get the best deal. We go via the local stationers, so that I can buy some CNY decorations to take home with me. I settle on a pair of small, beautiful lanterns, which I think will look lovely blowing in the summer breeze on the terrace at Puyssonier, in France.

We find a lovely small pot, just the right size for the space in the living room, and share the cost. From a nearby stall I add to my two lanterns with a mischievous-looking pair of red and gold monkeys. We finish our trip with a visit to the local phone shop for a simcard for me to use in one of Jay's iPhones while I am here. It's a more economical option than using my existing phone. As we are buying this, Jay phones to say he'll be home in half an hour, and 'What's the plan?' I've answered the phone as Keso is dealing with the purchase, and so can tell him that we are having drinks on a rooftop terrace somewhere before supper.

Jay is already home when we get back, and it's lovely to see him. There are technical conversations between them about the phone, and then Keso and I set off for what I now know to be Wooloomooloo – and that pre-supper drink, where Jay will join us. It's a three-minute walk from the apartment, then up to a modest 32nd floor, and we're out onto a terrace in the crisp night air of an indigo-sky Hong Kong, and a geography lesson from Keso – at my request – so that I can orientate myself. To the right is Happy Valley; further around to the right are the lights of the Bowen Trail, with Adventist hospital beyond. Back in front of us is the race track, and then sweeping around to the left, the harbour with its boats, and Causeway Bay. The dark night sky is dotted with the lights from windows in the buildings that sit beneath and alongside us, and that tower above us. There is a wonderful urban beauty to it all!

Wickedly, I indulge in two drinks: a gin and tonic with an orange flavour, and then a cocktail with a big hit of ginger. I don't care about how I might feel tomorrow; I'm celebrating being with a healthy daughter and having no responsibilities!

We walk to Causeway Bay for our Dim Sum supper at Din Tai Fung. I have forgotten how busy the streets of Hong Kong are in the evening, like Oxford Street at Christmas. This is added to by the daily arrival of people coming home to the island to celebrate Chinese New Year. The restaurant is very busy with people milling around holding numbered tickets, waiting to be seated. We take ours, and as we are discussing whether to stay or go elsewhere, we are approached by a young woman who asks us if we mind sharing a table. As we don't mind at all, she leads us through the packed restaurant to the perfect large round table, in what must be the quietest corner of the restaurant. We are sharing with three young men, but have plenty of space and a good vantage point from which to people-watch. The food is, as I expected, delicious, with dishes I have never eaten in the UK – and the bamboo steamers keep coming; *xiao long bao* (chicken and pork dumplings), steamed spinach with garlic, spicy pork and prawn dumplings, bean sprouts with minced pork…

I am very happy, very full and rather exhausted at the end of this first day back on the island, and looking forward to many, many more to come…

It's the last week of my stay here in Hong Kong, and, unable to put it off any longer, I begin my pilgrimage. Along the familiar streets of Wan Chai to Hopewell, up to the 17th floor and out onto Kennedy Road. I walk slowly, allowing the memories to unfold. On the street everything looks just the same, but within me so many changes. I climb the steep steps to the Wan Chai gap, and slowly, without looking up, begin my ascent. I am surprised, my legs remember this climb, and soon enough I find my rhythm, zigzagging my way up the sharp incline. This is a quiet time of day and I find myself walking alone. My body holds the blueprint for this walk, keeping me to a slow steady pace. At the point that I hear the pounding of my heart loud in my ears I look up, knowing instinctively that I have reached the top. Without stopping to catch my breath I walk to the pagoda and take a seat. This is where Anthony and I sat and talked and waited...

Today it is silent, no music, no gentle art of Tai Chi to soothe and distract, but it is not needed. Instead I select the music of Madeleine Peyroux to listen to as I complete my pilgrimage.

I walk the trail, softly singing along with the music. Wanting to dance, my body takes on a swaying lightness, my steps tracing the rhythms of her songs. At Lover's Rock, where shrines and statues to various deities are bathed in the sweet heady scent of burning incense, I hesitate; I look up and am reassured to see the incense seller-cum-shrine keeper in his place. As I walk on the path becomes busier. Young runners pass me in both directions, covered in Lycra, phones held firmly in place on arms, programmed to record kilometres covered, calories burned, steps taken, records broken. Filipino domestic workers walk dogs, chatting to friends at their side or on their phones. Elderly local ladies walk briskly in ones and twos and threes, talking and laughing. Elderly men run in Tee-shirts and shorts, a look of determination in their eyes. And in the background the ever-present sound of jackhammers and diggers, proclaiming Hong Kong's never-ending upward expansion. Here and there a lone banyan tree – marooned in the chaos of development – held firmly in place with an intricate criss-cross of cables, tagged and waiting to form the centrepiece of the new landscape. I reach the end of the trail, and where my companions turn around, ready to start their journey back, I turn and climb the short flight of steps to the pavement. Madeleine is singing 'This is Heaven to Me.'

Opposite me is the hospital, and as I stand and wait for my opportunity to cross the busy road, I read the large sign that in my three months of almost daily visits, I had never noticed:

Hong Kong Adventist Hospital and Heart Centre.

A steep flight of steps takes me to the hospital entrance. It occurs to me that my time at Adventist had been one of consistently and steadily ascending – of moving and progressing towards a higher level or degree. I feel joyful and light. I smile, and the greeter at the door nods and smiles back. In the reception area I pause to look about me, recognising faces, people busy at their work – *professionally serving, personally caring.* I wait for the lift to take me to the seventh floor... we approach the all-too-familiar third floor, but the lift doesn't stop. At my destination I head for the refectory, hot and thirsty after my climb. I buy a drink, remembering the many hours spent here. One last look around then I take the stairs back down to the ground floor, stopping to read once more the affirming statements underneath each picture on the wall at the bottom of each flight of steps. I am so engaged in this activity that I fail to notice that I have reached the basement. And there on the wall for the first time I read, 'You are never alone.' I retrace my steps, coming up from the darkness...

I leave the hospital still feeling joyful, light and full of love and hope. As I walk the curve of the drive that takes me back down to the road, I look up and read the large words mounted on the side of the hill – 'Extending the Healing Ministry of Christ'.

On my walk back along the Bowen Trail I stop at Lover's Rock and buy a set of incense sticks. With the lit incense firmly held outstretched between my hands, I wave them up and down as I bow three times to the statue of Brahma, the god who created knowledge and the universe. I place three sticks in each of the three incense pots in front of the shrine. Next, I visit the shrine of Kwan Yin, the goddess of mercy and compassion. Once more I bow three times:

Thank you for my daughter's life
Thank you for guiding me
Thank you for your love and protection
Thank you, thank you, thank you.

I place the remaining sticks in the pots before her, and continue my walk back to Keso, Jay and WanChai...

ABOUT THIS STORY

Stepping into a story is like stepping onto an escalator: it will carry you to a destination that you have selected – maybe familiar, perhaps unknown – but once you step off you have to move under your own momentum and find your own way; but with the story now inside of you…

Rather than the destination, it now becomes your travelling companion, and there are conversations to be had with it about those aspects that you found compelling reading, those that went straight to the heart of the matter, and those that you found problematic or ill advised.

According to the United Nations, world population reached seven billion on October 31st, 2011. The population of the UK as I write this in December 2015 is in excess of sixty-five million. It is clear to me that in my writing I will not please all of the people all of the time.

This story will have something useful to offer to some people, and hopefully they are the ones who will find it on the shelves in bookstores, online or through recommendation. I say *useful*, rather than *positive*, because I know I have learned as much from writers whose ideas immediately find a home in my heart and head, as from those whose ideas I find uncomfortable, unfamiliar and challenging, and in the moment seek to refute or reject.

I hope that you understand that this is not a tale of how to survive cerebral venous thrombosis and brain abscesses. I would hazard a guess that not even a qualified and experienced doctor would tell you how to do this; there are too many variables to factor in. But I think I could safely say that without doctors you would have no chance at all.

Albert Einstein observed that you cannot solve a problem from the same consciousness that created it. You must – if you like – take yourself to a new *viewing point* to see more fully. All that I am offering you – if like me life presents you with the unexpected and unwanted – is a chance to pull over on the journey and see things from a different perspective.

Einstein also said:

> A human being is a part of the whole called by us universe, a part limited in time and space. He experiences himself, his thoughts and feelings as something separated from the rest, a kind of optical delusion of his consciousness. This delusion is a kind of prison for us, restricting us to our personal desire and to affection for a few persons near to us. Our task must be to free ourselves of this prison...

In following what some might call my intuition, I sought to do exactly this. I was seeking to influence my daughter's state of health by tapping into the vast reservoir of energy that the universe offers us. Anyone familiar with the work of Lynne McTaggart – and her important book, *The Field* – will know that for a number of decades respected scientists have been carrying out experiments that challenge the Newtonian view of ourselves as separate and self-contained. What they have discovered, through scientific experiment, is that there may be such a thing as a life force flowing through the universe. As Lynne writes,

> Human beings and all living things are a coalescence of energy in a field of energy connected to every other thing in the world. This pulsating energy field is the central engine of our being and our consciousness.

Translating this to Keso's situation, in this place we were all connected in a communal process – doctors, nurses, friends, family, insurers, employers, strangers – we became a strong community with the good intention of seeing Keso returned to full health.

I had no way of knowing what would happen to my daughter. Would she continue in good health embodied as Keso? Would she be brain-damaged or otherwise impaired? Would she die and no longer be confined to a body, but return to an energetic state? Or would death be the end?

What I do believe is that connection, intention, medicine in all its forms, had their role to play in my daughter's recovery. Had she died I would have felt, like any other mother, the pain and anguish of losing a child. I would know also that I had done all that I believed I could do to support her, and over time would have found comfort in my understanding that Life doesn't end with death.

Lynne McTaggart wrote in *The Field*:

> As Fritz-Albert Popp described it, when we die we experience a 'decoupling' of our frequency from the matter of our cells. Death may be merely a matter of going home or, more precisely, staying behind – returning to the Field...

GRATITUDES & RECOGNITIONS

*'At times our own light goes out and is rekindled by a spark
from another person. Each of us has cause to think with deep
gratitude of those who have lighted the flame within us...'*
Albert Schweitzer

To name all the many wonderful people who supported us on this journey would call for the writing of another book. If you read this book you may recognise yourself in its pages, and know how much you are loved and how much we have to thank you for. If you sent us prayers, kind thoughts, healing energy, we thank you for it. If you sent us money, we thank you for it. To all the doctors, nurses and hospital staff who cared for Keso or had a role in her recovery, and showed us all such kindness and compassion, we thank you for it. To the distant healers holding us in the Light, we thank you. To staff at Lewis, thank you for your amazing, generous and compassionate support for a new member of staff not even in post for a month. To staff at Blue Cross, thank you for responding urgently to our anxious requests for reimbursement. To the ancestors and their appeal for healing, thank you for your hands in the small of my back. Family, friends and strangers have walked this unexpected road with us and in so doing eased our passage and lightened our load, and we are grateful to you all. My gratitude is twofold, for the gift of life for Keso and for the gift of experiencing that if you listen to your soul it will never lead you astray...

Be grateful for whatever comes
for each has been sent as a guide from beyond

Rumi

There are, of course, several people without whom the writing of this book would have been an overwhelming if not impossible task, and they must be named.

First and foremost, my amazing daughter Keso Kendall, who enthusiastically urged me to write, and who helped me to fill the gaps.

Jerome (Jay) Canlas for his photographs; for his invaluable daily chronicling of events, and for his amazingly detailed records around which I was able to weave my tale.

Anthony Kendall, my partner and co-parenter, for believing that I could do it and for drawing to my attention those events that I had omitted, but that were crucial to the authenticity of the story.

My daughter Tunde and grandson Buddy for taking on the care of gran-gran so that Anthony and I could be with Keso.

Karen Stefanyszyn, coach and friend, who freely gave of her time every fortnight, shining her light into my fears and limiting beliefs, so that I could move beyond them.

Julia Gray, our guardian angel of all things holistic, complimentary and editorial. Who spent a huge amount of time reading and editing and empowering.

Barbara Dryhurst, sister/friend, actor, and generous, wise reader, willing to share with me her knowledge of the *broken fourth wall where the audience are looking in so we need to stand and speak where they can see and get it.* And for generously letting me stay in her and Mark's beautiful home by the sea while I read and corrected the manuscript.

Delcia McNeil, healer, therapist, teacher, artist and published reader. So aware of how important the practical details are, and willing to spend time on making sure that I didn't overlook them.

Lynne Wilson, all-round wise woman, teacher and reader, always available to respond to my questions, my concerns, and to inspire me to believe in myself.

Gary Tywnam, author, whom I've never met, but who generously agreed to read my manuscript as a self-confessed, 'non-believer, conditioned mind, homeopath-denier, iconoclast and general unicorn-slayer'. Who provided me with feedback from 'the dark side' that was clear, direct, useful and surprisingly positive.

Christine King, founder and Principal of the Metaphysical Society for the Expansion of Consciousness, for making the principles that are becoming the foundation of my life available and accessible. And for generously agreeing to write the review.

To Simon Coury, actor, writer, proofreader and father, for finding time in his busy life to proofread this book.

My mother, Doreen Eytle, for being the grit in the oyster that keeps me searching for the pearl...

ABOUT THE AUTHOR

The two activities that have brought more joy, wisdom and peace into my life than I could ever have imagined, are weaving and working with metaphysical principles.

Weaving came into my life some forty years ago to anchor me, to connect me to the ancestors and to slow me down. It succeeded, and in so doing opened up an inner journey, which brought me to Metaphysics and the natural Laws of the Universe.

With these two to support me, life feels more like a pilgrimage, a transformative journey, with the Self as the destination. This sort of travelling has no end, but is rather a spiraling to a deeper awareness of what it means to live as a spiritual being having a human experience.

When I find myself struggling or in pain, I know that they will help me find a way through it, motivating me, lifting my spirits and filling me with the energy to move forward.

When I feel inspired, creative and joyful, it is because they have returned me to the truth of how wonderful Life truly is!

This is the first time that I have found the courage to write about what is in my heart.

73063516R10109

Made in the USA
Columbia, SC
04 July 2017